D0100105

COLLECTOR'S ENCYCLOPEDIA OF

EARLY NORITAKE

Aimee Neff Alden

COLLECTOR BOOKS

A Division of Schroeder Publishing Co., Inc.

The current values in this book should be used only as a guide. They are not intended to set prices, which vary from one section of the country to another. Auction prices as well as dealer prices vary greatly and are affected by condition as well as demand. Neither the author nor the publisher assumes responsibility for any losses that might be incurred as a result of consulting this guide.

On the cover:

A tea service in black, gold and white, with raised goldwork. Clockwise: teapot, sugar bowl, teacup and saucer, and creamer. Pattern 20056, shown on page 86.

Book Design by Karen Long
Cover Design by Beth Summers

Searching For A Publisher?

We are always looking for knowledgeable people considered to be experts within their fields. If you feel that there is a real need for a book on your collectible subject and have a large comprehensive collection, contact Collector Books.

COLLECTOR BOOKS
P.O. Box 3009
Paducah, KY 42002-3009

Copyright © 1995 by Aimee Neff Alden
Values Updated, 2000

All rights reserved. No part of this book may be reproduced, stored in any retrieval system, or transmitted in any form, or by any means including but not limited to electronic, mechanical, photocopy, recording, or otherwise, without the written consent of the author and publisher.

CONTENTS

Dedication to Betty Jean 4

Foreword by Richard R. Schleiger...5

Acknowledgments 6

Introduction 7

Understanding Backmarks..8

Section I

    Backmarks MM-1 through MM-16..10

    Patterns 1895 to 1916 13

Section II

    Backmarks MM-17 through MM-28..37

    Patterns 1917 to 1929 39

Section III

    Backmarks MM-29 through MM- 41...100

    Patterns 1930 to 1939 102

Section IV

    Backmarks MM-42 through MM-57...169

    Patterns 1940 to 1955 172

Old Noritake Patterns in Numerical Order..194

Cup Shapes and Sizes Found in Early Patterns...197

Evaluating Noritake China: The Price Guide 201

Appendix A:

    The Howard Kottler Collection 207

Appendix B:

    Historical Background of Chinaware in the United States...210

Bibliography..214

Dedication To Betty Jean

It was on the occasion of my ninth Christmas that Santa Claus brought me a perfectly beautiful baby doll — marking the beginning of my love affair with oriental porcelain. Many years later I discovered that Betty Jean, as I named the doll, was a Noritake product made in 1920. This information came from Patricia Smith, a doll authority and author of the book *Antique Collector's Dolls,* in which Betty Jean is pictured. I am confident that having this doll to play with and care for was an influence that, in later years, led me to undertake a thorough study of early Noritake patterns — which I had come to admire for their superb workmanship and elegant designs.

Betty Jean is featured here, and although unseen, bears the komaru mark (see backstamp MM-5C) on the back of her head. Considering the problems faced by the Noritake Company's founders associated with two world wars, it seems appropriate that this backstamp, issued in 1908, is the symbol for "the overcoming of difficulties" and was the clan crest or *mon* of the Morimura family.

It is to Betty Jean, who today looks out over the multifarious activities of my studio, that I dedicate this latest representation of my researches into Noritake china.

Aimee Neff Alden
Placerville, California

FOREWORD

Over forty years ago my mother, Arlene Schleiger, and I initiated a project that was to greatly assist those interested in French Haviland China. This project consisted of identifying and cataloging my mother's extensive collection of Haviland china and publishing a series of five volumes, *Two Hundred Patterns of Haviland China*. These books have made it possible for those suffering loss or damage in their own sets to identify their patterns accurately. Today our books constitute the "bible" for those interested in Haviland china — stimulating a new business, that of matching Haviland china.

Now Aimee Alden, who knew my mother, is here offering for early Noritake china owners and collectors a splendidly organized and illustrated guide to the identification of the oldest Noritake china patterns, bringing valuable assistance to owners, collectors and dealers — and adding significantly to the study of oriental porcelains. This book is a need well met.

Richard R. Schleiger

Richard R. Schleiger

❧

ACKNOWLEDGMENTS

My special thanks to my son, Roland Alden, for the superb photography displayed in this book, and to my husband, Roland H. Alden, for his encouragement and support of the project.

Thanks are due to Hiro Arikawa of the Noritake Company, Incorporated, in Compton, California, for putting me in touch with hundreds of owners of old patterns, who have generously provided material critical to this effort.

I want also to thank Diane Van Camp, who has worked long and faithfully as editorial assistant, the versatile Virginia Piazza, and the entire staff of The Matchmakers, Incorporated, for their able help.

The following friends, customers and buyers have provided samples of their own patterns which were photographed for inclusion in the book:

Sandy Arnett
Diane Ayers
Roberta Bailey
Bev Baker
Mrs. Phyllis Baldwin
Dorothy W. Barnett
Kathleen R. Baron
Mrs. Teresa Barton
Lee Bennett
Penny Berman
Elvera M. Bierlein
Mary Blair
Robert B. Blake
Mr. & Mrs. W. Bradley
Deanne S. Brooks
Thelma Brookens
Kathy Buss
Isabel Catogge
John J. Chandler
Susan Chapin
James Cleveland
Perry Cleveland
Mrs. Donna Courtwright
Chris Des Marais
Ann Doogan
Fran Driscoll
Mrs. Sam Feiwell
Susan S. Fossum
Karen Franklin
Mary D. Gale
Mrs. Robert Gorechi
Joy Green
Betty Halton
Lois Hardee
Elizabeth Harth

Betty Hauenstein
Harriet Grace Fryer Hauser
Christine Hefner
Susan Hirshman
Helena Hofer
Trudy Huber
Michael K. Hulsman
Kathy Hutson
Ruth Ilgen
Lynda Ireland
Mrs. Robert Irons
Walter Iverson
Margo Jenkins
Mrs. Joe Jilderda
Retha J. Joella
Mr. Jim Johnson
Lois Johnson
Jones and Herron
Jackie Kelley
Patricia Klauck
Pat Kosconski
Dee Lamonica
Rita Larson
Mrs. L. Lawson
John Lloyd
Margarita Luna
Joyce Lurtz
Fred Marsh
Florence McClain
Linda McMenimon
Dan Meek
Dr. Ruth Mills
Mrs. Michael Muir
Forest A. Oldenburg
Adele Peterson

M. Pettingill
Cath Posehn
Chris Prentice
Pat Pruitt
Mrs. Daniel D. Quinn
Mrs. Sylvia Rasmussen
Mrs. R. L. Raymer
Jerry Richards
Jane and Larry Rosen
Myra Rosenthal
Mary Roy
Barbara Rutter
Marcie Sanz
Pepper Schmuck
B.J. Schneider
Barbara Scibetta
Mrs. Pierce Sherman
Merlanne Smith
Sharon Snoke
Jean Stark
Margot Stengel
Doris Sutton
Mrs. Frank Tavaszi
Bonnie Thompson
Margaret T. Thompson
June J. Time
Barbara S. Tompkins
Mr. & Mrs. Mitchell M. Truitt
Jean Walsh
Susie Wasserman
Mrs. K. Wildfong
Pam Wood
Hedda Wright
Mrs. W. H. Young
Diane Ziet

INTRODUCTION

History is of the greatest interest when it has something of ourselves in it. Most people own tableware; many wonder about its origins, its uniqueness, its name — even its value — and do not know where to turn for help. The Matchmakers, Inc. grew out of efforts to assist the ever-growing number of you who have inherited, bought, collected or merely wish to own and use the increasingly popular dinnerware produced by the Noritake Company.

The fact that the manufacturer of this fine china reused old pattern names for postwar designs that were entirely different from the originals, adds enormously to the problem of supplying bona fide matches to those seeking to "fill out" Grandmother's china. Over the years, we have amassed what is quite probably the most complete file of information on, as well as stocks of, patterns about which very little is generally known.

This book's limited goal is to deal solely, but as fully as possible, with tableware produced by the company founded by the Morimura family between about 1891 and the 1950's, when today's familiar "N-in-wreath" trademark was adopted by the Noritake Company — and post-World War II exporting was resumed.

Prior to 1890, foreign wares were admitted into the United States without any indication of the country of origin. However, following enactment of the Tariff Act of 1890, imports from Japan were marked "Nippon." Many collectors, and not a few dealers, are unaware that the word "Nippon" does not identify a type of ware, a factory, or a pattern — but only signifies that the piece was made in Japan between the years 1891 and 1921. In the latter years a decree by the United States Treasury required that henceforth "Japan" be substituted for "Nippon"; yet, it must be remembered that china produced for domestic sale, or for export to countries other than the United States, was not bound by such restraints; indeed, it was not required that each piece of a set be stamped and, not uncommonly, removable paper labels were used in place of an incised or painted mark. Thus travellers, both civil and military, often return home with sets of china unusually marked, or not marked at all — sometimes leading to the belief (even misrepresentation) that something is old that, in fact, was just recently produced and handpainted to match an original.

This book is a compendium of patterns from an earlier work, *Early Noritake China* (Alden and Richardson) but includes results of my continuing research from 1987 to the present; of verifiable patterns of Noritake china designs created and sold by the Noritake company, beginning at the turn of the century and continuing to 1955.

Early Noritake China showed approximately 457 patterns in black and white, arranged alphabetically (or numerically), with their accompanying descriptive legends. This book presents 248 additional patterns, bringing up to date all information on Noritake patterns that I have verified and matched, with the added advantage that most of the illustrations are in color. It is my belief that this book provides information that will prove useful, if not indispensable, to owners, collectors, and matching services, due in part to the fact that the period it embraces was a time when hostilities led to the loss by the Noritake Company of most of its records.

Reader interest has convinced me to attempt an updated version, with the expansion of illustrations in color; encouragement has also come from the Noritake Company offices in the United States and the Noritake Service Center of Arlington, Illinois.

This book includes four sections which depict and discuss four significant time spans: Section I from 1895 through 1916; Section II from 1917 through 1929; Section III from 1930 through 1939; and Section IV from 1940 through 1955.

At the beginning of each Section, the reader will find the backstamps appropriate to the particular section followed by pattern illustrations — in alphabetical order if named, then numerically where only numbers are known. Finally there is a listing of patterns for which we have no firm information as to name or number. These have been designated Mystery Patterns and have been assigned arbitrary numbers; interruptions in the number sequence indicates that an official name and/or number has been found (the mystery has been solved!) and the pattern has been assigned to its proper Section.

The Sections are followed by Old Noritake Patterns in Numerical Order, Cup Shapes and Sizes Found in Early Patterns, and Evaluating Noritake China: The Price Guide.

In the appendices will be found the Kottler Collection and the Historical Background of Chinaware in the United States.

UNDERSTANDING BACKMARKS

The first step in identifying a particular Noritake china pattern is to study the backmark (backstamp) to be found on nearly every piece of the china, with the exception of saucers and smaller pieces, such as salt and pepper shakers. True backmarks, as we know them today, were for the most part nonexistent before 1904, when Nippon Toki Kaisha, Ltd., forerunner of the Noritake Company, was founded. The first backstamp was registered in 1908 for the domestic market. Some confusion arises from the fact that the Noritake Company added the words "Nippon Toki Kaisha" to the backmark of china produced much later (see MM-51), leading to the erroneous assumption that the presence of the words "Nippon Toki Kaisha" means the china is "old." Actually, this slogan roughly translates as "Japan's Finest China" and has nothing in common with early Nippon.

All the backstamps we have seen over many years are described and pictured in *Early Noritake China* by Alden and Richardson (1987) and each has been given an arbitrary Matchmakers' number. One may consult this source for a comprehensive list of backstamps, including many variations. In this volume we have listed and pictured only the basic marks, omitting numerous variants, since these do not play a significant role in determining the time frame for pattern production. As nearly as possible, the backmarks are placed in chronological order: all Section I patterns (backmarks MM-1 through MM-16) are placed first, Section II patterns (backmarks MM-17 through MM-28) next, followed by Section III patterns (backmarks MM-29 through MM-41). Section IV patterns (backmarks MM-42 through MM-57) closes the Section groupings.

Among the backmarks illustrated in Section I are a wide variety of marks, many of which are not represented on china samples included in this book, since we do not picture any patterns for which we lack an actual sample to provide verification. You will also note that the marks differ widely from each other — ranging from the MM-1 stamp, with a maple-leaf motif, to doughnut-shaped stamps, to the Royal Sometuke Nippon stamps (which do not include the word "Noritake"), to the komaru devices (which may or may not include the word "Noritake" as well as "Nippon" — and often include the words "hand painted").

You will also find demonstrated here (Section I) the first use of the wreath-shaped mark enclosing the letter "M" (standing for "Morimura"). Backmarks which include this wreath enclosing the letter "M" designate china manufactured prior to World War II; after the war, the "M" was replaced with an "N" (for Noritake) as illustrated in backstamps MM-58, 59, and 60. However, these "N" patterns fall in a time period beyond the scope of this book.

It will be useful at this point to clarify the import of the appearance in many backmarks of the words "hand painted." This is not to be interpreted that the entire piece has been hand painted; but rather that, while executed with the usual decals, it has been "hand-finished" — typically with gold or enameled areas. A piece completely hand painted would be unique, not a registered pattern, and therefore probably unmatchable.

A primary goal of this book is to help the users identify their own pattern — by name, number and/or year of manufacture. Beginning with the mark MM-10, and continuing through MM-26, the device most often used in the back-stamp is the wreath with one single leaf at its base extending somewhat into the wreath's center, pointing toward the "M." This basic back-stamp may be found in various colors; in addition to the "M" in wreath it may show the pattern name above the stamp, in block letters, or below it, with the pattern name enclosed in an elongated rectangle with pendants at either end. Also, it may say "Hand Painted Nippon," or "Hand Painted Japan," or "Made in Japan." It can also carry the "US Design Patented" logo, and sometimes has Arabic numbers indicating the patent number, or Japanese characters giving the registry number. Occasionally one may find the name of the retailer carrying the pattern or the factory decorating it (see MM-11 and MM-21).

Many stamps in the late 'twenties and very early 'thirties are found on china made for export to countries other than the United States (see MM-33). Beginning about 1933, the wreath mark is extensively used, but differing from the MM-10 mark, by the addition of extra branching laurel leaves at the bottom of the wreath, tied with a tiny bow-shaped ribbon. This same mark (as in MM-38) is also found with the same branching laurel leaves, but with a larger ribbon bow. MM-39 illustrates still another version of the wreath with a centered "M," but one surrounded by scrolls rather than leaves.

While in 1940 the "M-in-Wreath" found limited employment, by 1945 (with the ending of hostilities) new devices were developed for back-marks: the komaru mark, in a sophisticated version now known as the "spoke in wheel" and "spoke in scroll," made its appearance; and the "Rose China" marks found at this time and usually signifying a product of transitional quality, much of which carried the notation "Made in Occupied Japan."

In 1953 the old familiar wreath mark, with the large bow, appears, but with the centered "M" replaced by the "N" (for Noritake) — a mark still in use today.

A brief comment is needed about the pattern numbers which appear in many of the backstamps: US Design Patent Numbers were issued after a patent was granted; in early patterns, these are usually five digit numbers. The three and four digit numbers are the Japan registry numbers. The design patent and registry numbers are peculiar to the patterns on which they occur.

MM-1

MM-2

MM-2A

MM-3

MM-4

MM-5A

MM-1. Issued in 1891 and registered in Japan in 1911. This stamp appears in both green and blue, the green denoting first grade and blue second grade. It shows the word "Nippon" in conformance with the McKinley Tariff Act of 1890, requiring all imports into the United States to be marked with the country of origin.

MM-2. Issued in 1906, Japanese registry in 1911, and issued for wares destined for export to the United States. Found in both green and blue. The RC stands for Royal Crockery.

MM-2A. Issued in 1906, but for the domestic market. This round RC mark is found in magenta on the pattern The Mikado.

MM-3. Issued in 1906 for both domestic and foreign markets. "Sometuke" means "blue." The bat-shaped design is a good luck symbol. In bright blue.

MM-4. Royal Sometuke in bright blue. "Sicily" is the pattern name.

MM-5A. Issued 1906 to 1908 in a faint blue. The mark is known as "komaru," an Oriental term meaning "overcoming difficulties." It is also known as the "tree crest" mark, the clan crest of the Morimura family. This mark and its variants were used for china destined for export to the United States.

MM-5C   MM-6   MM-7

MM-8   MM-9   MM-10

MM-5C. This version of MM-5 was impressed on the back of the neck of my Noritake doll.

MM-6. Both United States and Japanese registry in 1911. This mark is the first appearance of the "M-in-wreath" mark, the "M" standing for Morimura. Found in green, blue, gold and magenta.

MM-7. A Royal Crockery stamp registered in Japan in 1911 for export to the United States.

MM-8. 1911 Japanese registry in blue-black. Sometimes sold as whiteware to decorating studios.

MM-9. Issued in 1908 for export to England with Japanese registry in 1911. The "tree crest" mark appears in a more stylized form in bright turquoise blue. Variants may have Japanese characters and pattern numbers in red, with the mark itself in green.

MM-10. Issued in 1912. All printing in red, balance of stamp green.

MM-11

MM-12

MM-13

MM-14

MM-15

MM-16

MM-11. Circa 1912–1922. Our continuing research has shown this backstamp is a variant of MM-10 and also MM-19, MM-21 and MM-22 and, since these all occupy the same time slot, they may be grouped together.

MM-12. Backmarks in this category came in many color variants.

MM-13. Between 1912 and 1922. Variants include different color treatments.

MM-14. Circa 1916 in pale blue. It appears on two Noritake patterns, Azalea and Monterey.

MM-15. Circa 1915–1919. An early backmark, in pale green.

MM-16. Circa 1921. Bright blue.

You will see that these very early old favorites are not typical of the patterns made in later years. They include several with distinctly oriental characteristics (see Blue Willow, Rouen and Berkeley) and others with a more European look (see The Bosnia, The Crete and Mystery 124), setting them apart from designs made later to appeal especially to the American market.

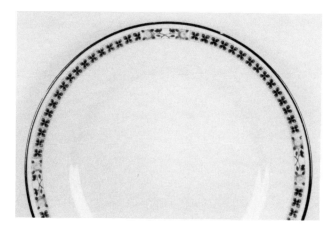

ALAIS (The) MM-12, MM-22. Gold edge, blue border of stylized flowers with insets of rose-colored roses with green leaves. Tan lines above and below border.

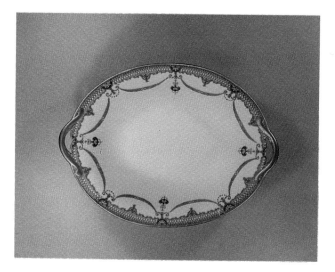

ALBANY MM-12, MM-22. Gold edge, mustard yellow border with deep blue dots and background of a half flower. Swags of yellow-green with pendants of deep blue, mustard and yellow.

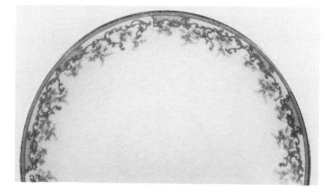

ALSACE (The) Mark 12 B. Gold edge. Fern green narrow band and below that a lemon yellow background interspersed with tan cross-hatching. A garland all around of pink roses and tiny blue flowers with green stems and leaves. Center all white. There is also a no-name pattern like this except blue instead of green, which is Mystery 123, MM-10.

ANGORA (The) MM-12. Gold edge, border of black with gold geometric design of circles and dots.

ANSONIA MM-13, MM-19. Cream border banded with tan lines. Insets of pink roses with blue background behind tan scrolls. A few pale green leaves. Line below border is gold, as is edge.

ARGONNE (The) MM-12. Gold edged geometric design with spring green scallops and dots with black and yellow touches. A violet wreath with yellow squares.

ARLEIGH 61234 MM-15, MM-22. Gold edge, delicate border in pink, blue and yellow floral, with green and yellow scrolls and leaves.

AZALEA MM-14, MM-19, MM-40. Pattern often found with no name and just the number 19322. Later back-stamps may include the number 252622. Large pale pink and white flowers with yellow stamens and red shafts. Gray-green and yellow-green leaves with touches of dark bottle green between flowers. Gold edge and gold behind the largest group of flowers. This is the well-known Larkin premium pattern.

BERKELEY MM-10. All white background with large and colorful oriental style design. Narrow soft blue border overlaid with an X-shaped motif in brown. Floral motifs alternate with large mushroom shaped designs, primarily Chinese red. Large central floral. This pattern has a brown edge rather than gold, and appears to be the same pattern as Derby.

BEVERLY MM-12. Dark blue and dark tan border inset with medallions. Gold edge, all white center. Not the same as Beverly 58589 which is also an old pattern pictured in Section II.

BLUE WILLOW 11006 MM-3, MM-16. Rich Sometuke blue on pure white ground. Note the two figures on the bridge. Worth collection. See also 16033, also a blue willow but not the typical blue willow.

BOSNIA (The) MM-12. No border other than the gold edge. Free flowing design of pink roses touched with yellow. All white background.

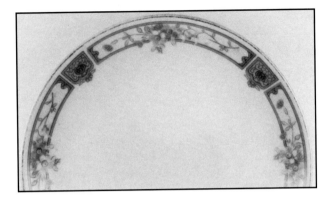

CARMEN 14370 MM-12. Also MM-19 variant with Japanese characters surrounding mark. Gold-edged narrow border pattern entirely outlined in mustard. Wide bands enclosing pale and bright pink roses with yellow centers, small bright blue flowers and pale green leaf sprays. These alternate with small insets of a different design in pale pink, yellow and bright blue, against a pale blue ground.

CEYLON (The) 58581 MM-12, MM-22. Mustard colored border of scrolls and insets of a single rose on black background, joined by a narrow band of "tongs" in dull green with touches of pink, yellow and black. Gold edge and inner line.

CRETE (The) MM-10 (a Noritake Nippon mark.) Geometric border of green, red and black. The Crete found in Section II is more usually found but it is different and slightly more recent than this one.

DERBY MM-10. Same pattern as Berkeley. Brown edge. Band of striped lozenges outlined in brown against a sky blue ground. Below this are large pink and yellow camellias, buds and green leaves alternating with an oriental motif outlined in brown, with touches of Chinese red, and also a mushroom design mostly in tan shades. This pattern is identical to Berkeley shown earlier but in color.

ELEANOR (BASSETT) MM-13. Delicate border with gold edge and two different pink floral motifs on a cream band. All white center.

FERNCROFT MM-10. Gold edge. White space. Medium brown band with black line centered within it. Carnation pink roses with olive green leaves and ferns form a part of the border band. All white background. There is a Bavarian pattern that matches Ferncroft exactly.

FLAMENGO (The) Mark MM-12. Brown edge. A handsome overglaze enamel pattern with a dull green scalloped outer border. Wide band of large, oriental-type stylized flowers in rose, yellow and blue, with leaves in brown-green. Large central design in same colors. An early pattern.

FORMOSA (The) MM-12. There is also a variant of this mark which does not say "Made in Japan." Gold edge. Greenish-yellow band and medallions with gray band below that surrounds the ½" border of carnation pink, maroon and yellow flowers with green leaves and gray branches. All white center. See Kottler watercolor designs in Appendix I (figure 3).

LINWOOD (The) MM-13. Delicate border, gold edged. Narrow white band with pale pink, yellow and lavender flowers and green leaves. A wider cream band below is edged on both sides with a tan pen line. White center.

HOWO MM-3, MM-25. Sometuke blue on white. Large flying phoenix birds and roses in overall design with a geometric border.

KIVA (The) MM-12. Reddish brown edge. Narrow diaper band of blue on blue. Inner pattern has 2 different designs overglaze enameled in bright rose, orange-yellow and blue with scrolls of foliage in yellow-green, gray-blue. Second design is yellow-green. Narrow scroll band below in blue and yellow. Central floral repeats same colors.

HAKONE 11298 MM-12, MM-22. Delicate old pastel pattern of stylized flowers, pink and white with pale yellow centers, green leaves and brown stalks "growing out" of an inner gold line. All white ground, gold edge.

LORRAINE (The) MM-13. Delicate border pattern, gold edged. Narrow cream band with roses in pink, rose and white, with yellow-green leaves connected by a pale beige thorny stem. Mystery 84 goes well with this as a substitute.

LUZON (The) MM-12, MM-19. Gold edge, narrow border of pink roses and blue flowers, green leaves and tiny blue and red buds. These alternate with a mustard border design on a pale blue background.

MAGENTA (The) MM-12, MM-22. Border is formed of white-grounded magenta and yellow-orange large flowers, interrupted with black reserves holding blue flowers.

MALAY (The) 13857 MM-12, MM-22. Gold edge. Border of white diamonds with a touch of orange-yellow. Cadet blue bands outline border of roses and blue flowers with green leaves. Then, alternating blue and tan medallions enclose another pink rose and small blue flowers. Entire body white.

MANDARIN MM-11, MM-22. Gold edge, oriental style pattern, full of color, to a gold pen line. Cream band 1" wide with two different Japanese planters, one in blue and green, other planter yellow with touches of black, dark blue and lavender. Inside are flowering branches in magenta, deep blue, orange, pink and dull red. Also, small bright butterflies of yellow.

MARGUERITE MM-13. A delicate floral border, gold edge, cream background to gold pen line. A pink and blue rose with green leaves are connected by a light tan vine of small pink roses and blue flowers. White center. Do not confuse with later Noritake pattern 6730.

MARNE (The) MM-10. Gold edge. Forget-me-not blue, corn flower blue, green-gray and pale yellow border. Cream band to light brown pen line that connects pale lavender, yellow and white flowers with light green leaves. Center is all white.

METZ (The) MM-10. Gold edge and inner line. Narrow border pattern of diagonal connecting stripes, one in yellow and black alternating with one in pale gray-blue. Above and below stripes are tiny pink roses with green leaves. White center.

MIKADO (The) MM-2, MM-8, MM-12. Smooth gold band ⅛" wide and gold pen line where rim joins the plate. Entire pattern gold and white.

MONTEREY (The) 58595 MM-12, MM-14. Gold edge. Narrow band encircling plate encloses sprays of oriental-type flowers in deep yellow and blue with blue-gray leaves and brown stems. Alternating insets in same colors.

ORIENTAL (The) No backstamp on our sample saucer. Brick red edge above a narrow yellow-orange band. Bright green-blue border with violet scrolls and pink chrysanthemums. Smaller motifs have touches of red. Large flowers, leaves and scrolls below the border are in brilliant oriental colors. This is a very old hand-painted pattern.

PAGODA (The) Mark 10. Gold edge. Oriental house and bridge in brick red and tan with olive green trees. Gold pen line below.

PHOENIX BIRD 10733 MM-3. Joan Collett Oates calls this pattern Twin Phoenix. Pattern is all intense dark blue on a white ground. Border of half-circles and below this is a 1" band of birds and flowers.

PORTLAND 13673 MM-12. First border of black and white squares beneath gold edge. Below this gray-blue scrolls on a tan-dotted background top the major border of roses, with insets of a pink rose centering a medallion. A black beaded chain is below the rose border. Entire background white.

PRINCETON MM-12. Gold edge, wider smooth gold band outlined by black lines and an inner gold pen line below. All white back-ground. Not same as Princeton 6911, a later pattern not included in this volume.

REGINA 13674 MM-12, MM-13, MM-22. Gold edge. Border design in shades of maroon, light pink, rose, black and moss green, with moss green and yellow bars below. Insets of pink roses and green leaves are also in the border design. White center.

ROUEN MM-13. An oriental style pattern with gold edge, light blue outer band edged in a gold pen line. Major central floral is pink, orange, yellow and blue with violet berries, brown stem and green leaves. Smaller florals on plate rim repeat these colors. All white background.

SAHARA (The) 58590 MM-12, MM-19, MM-22. Tan and black border, narrow band of yellow below. Lincoln drape and pink roses with central motifs in yellow, black and tan. All white background. Gold edge and a gold pen line at bottom of plate rim.

SEDAN (The) 11292. MM-13 and MM-19. Gold edge, narrow cream-colored band with handpainted pink and blue flowers with yellow centers and black dots, blue buds, pale green and blue foliage. A delicate early pattern.

SEVILLE 58584 MM-13, MM-19. Gold edge, black and white geometric border with insets of a small design consisting of one pink rose with green leaves and stem on a lavender background. Below this an ivory band ends with a gold pen line. Same design as Chanossa, colors different.

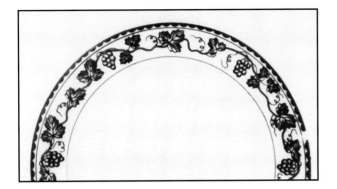

SICILY MM-4. Entire pattern intense dark blue on white. Tiny scallops at outer edge and then a border of grapes and grape leaves with connecting stems.

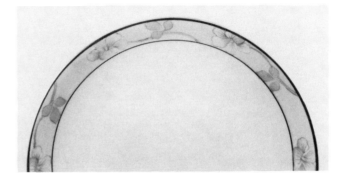

VALENCIA I MM-13. Gold edge. Border of large lavender flowers alternating with large, pale green leaves all outlined with tan. Tan line separates this border on a cream background from the white center. This is a version of the following Valencia 11632, but its border is narrower and there is no gold beading on edge.

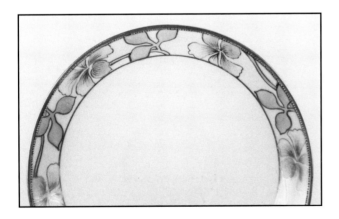

VALENCIA II 11632 MM-6 in magenta. Gold edge with raised beading and with pattern wider than on previous pattern and outlined in gold, not tan.

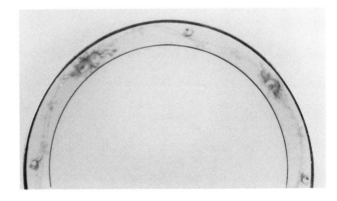

VENDOME MM-13. A delicate border pattern with gold edge and inner line. A half-inch band in pale cream encloses a pale, thorny vine in mustard-yellow with groups of pink and blue roses and buds, yellow-green foliage and pale blue shadow foliage. White center.

VITRY (The) 13672 MM-13, MM-19. Early delicate border pattern with gold edge against a narrow cream band. Pink roses and green leaves have yellow scrolls beside and beneath, and the smaller motif has a pale blue background.

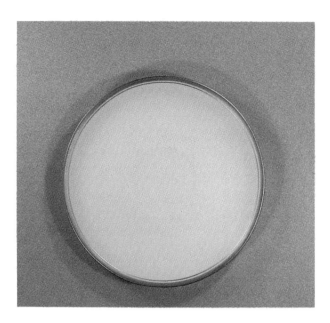

WAVERLY MM-12. Gold band and immediately below it a gold pen line on an all white body. Can be successfully intermixed with other gold band and line china such as Haviland.

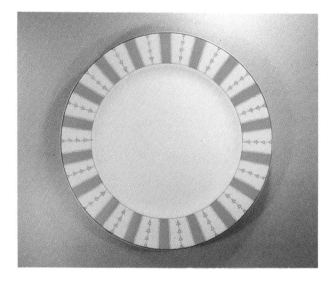

YALE (The) MM-13. Yale blue solid verticals alternating with verticals of bellflowers and dots on white. Entire pattern blue and white, no gold trim.

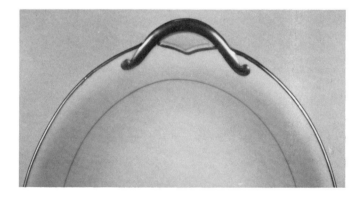

YUKON (The) MM-12. An all white body with gold banding and line.

9488 MM-16. Large flowers and leaves all in rich dark blue on white ground. No gold edge.

10733 MM-3. See also Phoenix Bird occurring earlier in the text. All in two shades of blue.

11006 MM-16. A typical Blue Willow design, all in rich blue on white background.

13680 MM-13. This pattern often not numbered on the piece. Groups of pink flowers enclosed by long scrolls separated with yellow single flowers and scroll-work with a diamond shaped motif and a pink flower centering the diamond.

16033 MM-3 and MM-16. Another typical Blue Willow design in rich dark blue on white.

16034 MM-5, MM-19. Beaded gold edge and entire pattern is gold, cream and white, with gold designs raised. Cream background to gold line and then white center. Some pieces are found with numbers reversed (43061) and some are marked 175 (MM-27, MM-48). Piece pictured is a berry bowl.

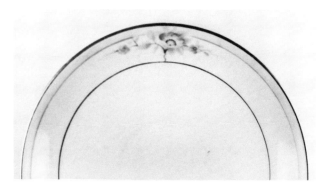

MYSTERY 4 MM-13. Narrow ivory band down to tan line. Gold line about 1" from edge. Pink open flowers.

44318 MM-9. Cream, gold and white pattern with the gold embossed. Cup differs from saucer in that the cup has a gold basket with floral sprays, while the saucer has a seven-pointed star.

MYSTERY 6 MM-15. Gold edge. Border of tiny yellow-green daisies and leaves in pearl gray on a yellow-green background. Pastel multiflorals and medallions alternate on the cream background to a gray pen line. White center.

MYSTERY 8 MM-15. Gold edge. Scalloped. Yellow, blue-green and black border design. Bouquets of flowers in deep yellow, light blue and pink, tinged with maroon. Large green leaves. Florals are on a cream background to inner blue-green scroll line. White center.

MYSTERY 12 MM-10. An oriental type pattern. Gold edge. Basic color in border is blue with bright florals. There are variants of Mystery 12, one of which has central large floral like the center bouquet in Rouen (see alphabetical listing).

MYSTERY 16 MM-12. Gold edge, all white piece. Gold pen lines on the handles and at the base. There is a narrow band of bright cornflower blue overlaid with a white floral wreath touched with bittersweet, pale yellow and yellow-green leaves.

MYSTERY 17 MM-12. Gold edge. Orchid and carnation pink violets touched with yellow. Green spring foliage, outlined occasionally with brown. All on white.

MYSTERY 40 MM-1 in blue. Chinese red edge. Narrow border in pale dull green. An early bird pattern in very bright colors. Wide border of pink oriental flowers with yellow centers, bright green leaves and tan branches. Peacocks in blue and yellow. A central floral motif repeats these colors. Background is white.

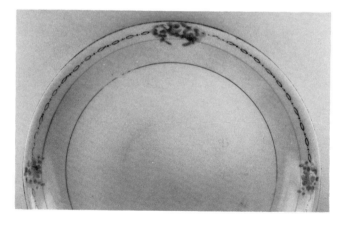

MYSTERY 41 MM-1. Gold edge. Narrow border of white with ovals in black and insets of small pink roses. Inner band is cream to the gold pen line. White center. A delicate border pattern.

MYSTERY 42 MM-15. Gold edge and light blue half-circles with black dots form geometric border design. Ivory background on plate rim, with oriental style floral groupings, ends in a wreath of yellow scrolls and multi-colored small flowers dividing the ivory section from the white center.

MYSTERY 51 MM-9. Gold edge and raised gold beading and outlines to bright green-yellow edge design. Pale pink, peach and white flowers, outlined in raised gold; pale blue, gold and light green scrolls connect the flowers. All on white background with flower group in center.

MYSTERY 52 MM-13. Gold edge. Delicate border of pink and white roses with pale blue and light green leaves connected by a green vine bearing blue and green leaves. All on a white background.

MYSTERY 60 MM-13. Gold edge. Ivory band to gold line. A delicate floral border in multicolors is dominated by a large pink rose connected by a gray vine. All white center.

MYSTERY 63 MM-1. Gold edge. Wide cream band edged in brown, with light pink, dark rose and lavender florals with green leaves separating sections of the band. Balance of the plate is white. A delicate border pattern.

MYSTERY 65 MM-15. Gold edge, tan scalloped narrow band. Below this is a light orange-yellow and black band. Cream background with pastel hand-painted flowers in light pink, green and lavender, with yellow scrolls. Yellow and black leaf motif edges the white center.

MYSTERY 66 MM-13, MM-19. Gold edge. A pale ivory band overlaid with delicate floral pattern of pink flowers and green leaves.

MYSTERY 69 MM-13. Gold edge. A half-inch border of green vine edged in black, with one stylized design in lavender and yellow and another of pink roses and green leaves. Pale lavender shadow foliage. See Kottler watercolors in appendix, figure 5.

MYSTERY 70 MM-12. Gold edge. All white background. An early pattern touched with enamel. Delicate wreath of orange, pink, blue and yellow flowers, and green leaves. Inner geometric band is fern green and yellow.

MYSTERY 73 MM-7. Wide gold edge and cream band to gold inner line. A delicate floral wreath on white ground near the center is accented by bright pansies in yellow, blue and magenta. A saucer is pictured.

MYSTERY 81 MM-6. Entire pattern cream, gold and white. Gold beading on edge; gold roses on cream background. White center.

MYSTERY 83 MM-10. Yellow edge with narrow aqua band of diamonds and flowers in lavender and yellow. Inner pattern encircling plate in pink, yellow, orange and aqua with green leaves. Same floral design in center. Identical design to Tokio, but colors are different.

MYSTERY 84 MM-13. Gold edge. Delicate border. Cream band edged below in tan. Border design of pale lavender thorny rose vines with inserts of a pink, white and pale yellow rose with green leaves and pale lavender shadow foliage.

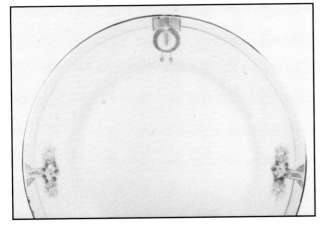

MYSTERY 96 MM-1. Gold edge. Pale cream band with tan inner pen line broken by two motifs — a pea-green geometric edged in tan, alternating with a combination of this design with added pink, white and yellow flowers, and green leaves. Lavender shadow foliage.

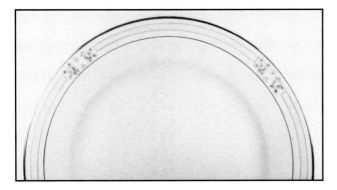

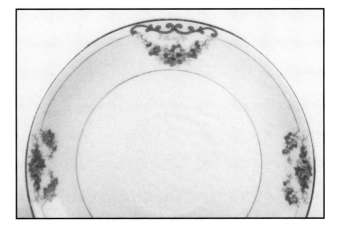

MYSTERY 97 MM-13. Gold edge. Narrow cream bars are edged in tan and separated by a motif of two pink roses and two small blue flowers with green leaves. A gold pen line beneath border. Entire background white. A delicate floral border.

MYSTERY 99 MM-12. Gold edge and gold pen line one-fourth inch from edge, then a cream background to inner line. A dull green-brown scroll surmounts a floral swag of pink and yellow roses with green leaves. Alternating florals in the same colors do not have the prominent scroll atop. A delicate border.

MYSTERY 104 MM-10, MM-19. Gold edge. A delicate border. Narrow cream band, then a white band ending with a green pen line. On the white band, two motifs of a pink rose with green leaves alternate.

MYSTERY 106 MM-2. Scalloped and on an embossed blank, possibly European. All lines and beading are heavy gold. Wide gold edge, then a pale yellow band. Surrounding the pattern, hand-painted within boxes of heavy overglaze blue ground, are designs in pink and magenta, with some green, cream, yellow and white. Inner narrow band of gold circles on a pale pink background. Design in center in pink, magenta, green and deep yellow.

MYSTERY 111 MM-7. Entire pattern outlined in gold and with gold beading. Delicate tiny flowers in orange and blue with pale green leaves. Picture is of the top of a pedestal salt which shows the pattern in good detail.

MYSTERY 120 MM-5. Raised gold beading on a pale ivory band. Between florals is a pale green motif. Helena Hofer collection.

MYSTERY 121 MM-12. Birds and butterflies in soft colors alternate with floral sprays. The geometric is black and blue and the plate is encircled with gold. Jones and Herron collection.

MYSTERY 122 MM-12. White background, gold edge, with butterflies and florals outlined in dark green forming the border. Collection of Mrs. Robert Irons.

MYSTERY 123 MM-10. This pattern appears to be the same as The Alsace, except this one is blue where Alsace is green.

MYSTERY 124 MM-8. One-fourth inch gold does not wrap the edge.

MYSTERY 125 MM-15. Large scrollwork in jade green and yellow, with typical florals. Black scallops beneath the gold edge.

MYSTERY 126 MM-15. Sky blue border edged in yellow and mustard scrolls. Typical Noritake bouquets on cream background. Prentice collection.

MYSTERY 181 MM-12. White china with gold band and line. Very similar to The Mikado but gold line is closer to edge.

MYSTERY 184 MM-9. *(left)* Gold edge, scenic view of a gray mountain peak with a bird in colors of black and orange with a touch of red in its topknot. Bamboo trees are dark brown and brown-green with gold accents. See also the Charles Field Haviland small saucedish *(right)* showing same general decor as Mystery 184 and illustrating how one manufacturer draws inspiration from another company. Both the Noritake and the Haviland pieces are from the same era.

MYSTERY 183 MM-15. Gold edge. One-fourth/inch border is Alice blue overlaid with cream and white scrolls. Ivory background to aqua line. Muticolored floral bouquets alternate with an elaborate vase, scroll and leaf design in yellow and blue. From the collection of Mrs. Judson W. Barton, whose mother received it as a gift from members of the Japanese community of Bayonne, New Jersey, in thanks for a kindness she did for them.

MM-17

MM-18A

MM-19

MM-20   MM-21   MM-21G   MM-22

MM-17. Issued 1916–1920. Comes in dull green. A forerunner of the well-known "cherry blossom" stamp (see MM-20).

MM-18A. Circa 1918. This shows the first use of the pattern name in a rectangle with pendent bellflowers, a familiar Japanese decorative device known as "kikyo."

MM-19. Circa 1918. Noritake made many variants of this stamp and it was used, with modifications, until the closing of the New York office of the Noritake Company in 1941. It came in a variety of colors, but this green backstamp was used on patterns decorated at the main factory at Nagoya.

MM-20 Circa 1925. A redesigned version of MM-17 and in the same dull green.

MM-21. Circa 1917–1925. See *Early Noritake China* by Alden and Richardson for variants made for Bassett, James China, and Marshall Field.

MM-21G. Since this mark appears on more than one pattern, we must assume that it represents a decorating company or distributor.

MM-22. Registered in Japan between 1921 and 1924. There are some 16 variants of this stamp, appearing in various colors, and usually including the pattern name.

MM-23

MM-24

MM-25

MM-26

MM-27

MM-28

MM-23. Registered in 1924. The cherry blossom logo was used on a large group of wares produced for United States import. It came in red, green, or blue, with decoration done by independent subcontractors. MM-23, Elmonte, does not bear the Noritake designation, but the same pattern appears on the marked Noritake and with the same United States patent number and name.

MM-24. An early mark, circa 1918–1920. Nagoya was the city where Noritake's main factory was located, and the N & Co. probably stands for Noritake Company. The crown above was a Noritake device and patterns with this backstamp may have been made for the domestic market or for export to countries other than the United States.

MM-25. A mark from about 1916, in bright blue. "Howo" is the Japanese name for the bird of paradise.

MM-26 Since it only says "Japan," it probably was issued about 1918. All in red. MM-26A has, in addition, a rectangle all in gold. Most gold, cream and white patterns had backstamps executed in gold.

MM-27. This stamp was used in 1930 and shows a new pattern number (#175) for the old favorite 16034. Both stamp and pattern are executed in gold.

MM-28 An early stamp, but after 1921; executed in bright blue, and possibly subcontracted.

PATTERNS 1917 TO 1929

These patterns are for the most part designs with a
geometric border. The backstamps number 17 through 28.

ADAMS MM-22. Border of yellow verticals touched with
black. Elaborate vase and scroll below in the same colors.

ADRIAN MM-22 variant. Gold edge. Leaf green and white
border surrounded by a narrow gold pen line. Multicolor
flower groups on cream background to gold line. White center.

AEOLIAN 76841 MM-22. Gold edge. Green stylized
border and elaborate wide green inner band. Orange, yellow, rose and blue floral arranged over a maize scroll on a
cream background incorporates a small blue bird.

ALICIA 35762 MM-22. Gold edge. Light tan border
with forest green bars and black dots and outlines.
Reserves in border hold pink, blue and tan small flowers. Cream background to inner circle that repeats motifs
in border design. Superimposed on cream are sprays of
dark pink roses, blue chrysanthemums and yellow
daisies alternating with green scrolls. See Raleigh, a similar pattern which could be mixed in with Alicia.

ALLERTON MM-22. See Rochambeau 61228. Same pattern as Rochambeau, but white background.

AMARILLO MM-22. Gold edge and immediately below a geometrical design in green and black surrounds the plate. Cream background on which are floral motifs ending in a scalloped scroll demarcating the white center.

AMERITA MM-19. Cadet blue and white rope border, then typical oriental flowers on the cream ground to white center.

AMISTON 69540 MM-22. Gold edge. Tiny white dots on a black ground, then a cream band ⅜" wide ending in an encircling design edged in small scallops and enclosing orange-yellow bars and cadet blue triangles, with vertical black lines and dots. An orange-yellow urn outlined in black holds blue scrolls and yellow leaves and is topped with a spray of pink roses. Below this design the white background about 1" wide ends in a gold pen line.

AMOROSA 78048 MM-22. Gold edge, tiny white circles on black ground with goldenrod insets in scalloping. Below this is a spring green band. Cream background to scrolling of green, yellow and black. Atop the cream band are bouquets in a yellow urn. Flowers in the urn are touched with enamel. The pattern named Carltonia has the same number.

ANACONDA MM-22. Gold edge. White, black and green border of geometric figures and an arrangement of gray feathers in a black and white vase. Cream background to center black line.

ANAMOSA MM-22. Gold edge with mustard border and baskets of blue and yellow fruits in reserves. Narrow inner band is cream, ending in a blue line, and below that a white band to gold line.

ANDALIA 83366 MM-18. Tan border design with tiny black scallops on which are superimposed olive green leaves and scrolls and small yellow and green circles. Cream background to black line, interrupted with insets of floral bouquets with a maize scroll beneath.

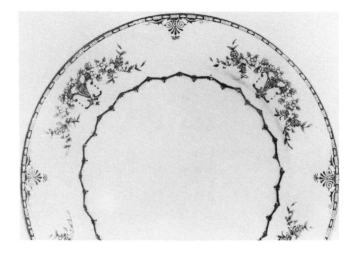

APOLLO 76833 MM-22. Gold edge. Black and maize border of rectangles and ovals. Florals and fruit in a brown urn are yellow, pink, blue, rose and green and are arranged on the cream background to a maize inner scroll.

ATHLONE 80460 MM-22. Gold edge. Cadet blue and yellow border. Flower groups, separated by a black line at the plate rim, are rose, apricot and blue, with green leaves.

AUSTIN MM-19. Gold edge. Gray geometric border and below this a cream band with insets of medallions and swags connected by a line demarcating the beginning of the white center. From the collection of Dr.

AVRIL MM-22. Gold edge, cornflower blue, mustard and black border of scrolls, bars and scallops ¼" wide. Cream background to the circle of scrollwork demarcating the white center. On the cream ground bouquets of goldenrod, bittersweet and sky blue flowers with fern green leaves. The inner circle is made up of black scallops, a mustard band, and pale blue half flowers.

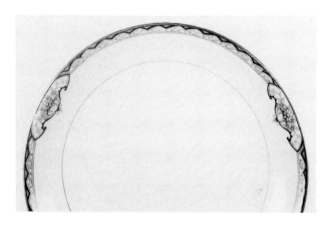

BANCROFT MM-22. Gold edge. Brown, black and white border with ½" cream band below it. Designs of yellow wreaths with brown scrollwork spaced on the cream. White center. Pattern is identical to Chanesta except that Chanesta is in shades of blue.

BARODA 68596 MM-22. Scallops and outlines of the floral insets are blue with yellow-orange below the scallops to the first narrow band. Cream background to inner charcoal pen line. White center. Floral reserves in border are yellow, orange and blue.

BASEL (The) 68466 MM-22. Black and tan geometric border with reserves holding a container of pink flowers. A gold edge. From the collection of Robert Blake.

BEAUMONT 69534 MM-19. Gold edge. Yellow and black border interrupted by blue wreath and ribbon, pink roses, green leaves and swags.

BEDFORD 68443 MM-22. Gold edge. Cream band ⅜" wide, then a burnt sienna band with black verticals and figures. Light pink and rose open roses with green leaves and stems form part of the border, extending into a white band that ends in a gold pen line.

BEECHMONT MM-19. Gold edge. Narrow geometric border in black on white with a delicate pattern of pink roses and green leaves on a black grounded inset. Gold inner line.

BELLEFONTE 68587 MM-22. Gold edge. Yellow figures on a tan band, then pale pastel flowers and medallion on a cream background. A gold pen line separates border from all white center.

BELLEFONTE 69539 MM-22. Gold edge. Geometric border in cornflower blue, leaf green and moss green, black lines and white dots. Medallions of black dots, blue swags and dots, centered with a red and yellow flower on a black background. A narrow cream band to black line, then narrow white band to gold line.

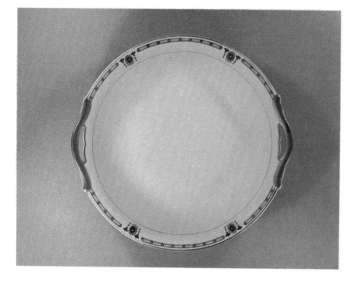

BEVERLY 58589 MM-22. Gold edge. Blue medallions around rim joined by a narrow border edged in tan, with insets of blue diamonds.

BIARRITZ 78047 MM-22. Yellow-orange, cadet blue and black border. Typical Noritake florals top a fan motif.

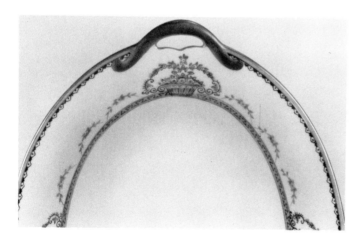

BLENKHEIM MM-19. Gold edge, tan band. Beneath this is a tiny black and gray-blue design. Brown, yellow and blue basket sits on a mustard and black inner band and holds blue, yellow and pink flowers. All design is on the cream background.

BORDEAUX MM-19. Gold edge, all white background. A wide border of blue geometric designs enclosing alternating green leaves with red berries and a decorative yellow motif and below that a fine gold penline. From the collection of Jane and Larry Rosen.

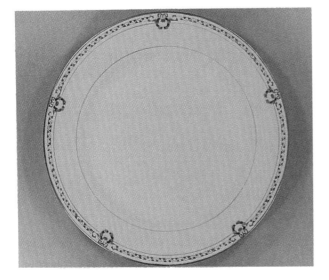

BRIARCLIFF MM-19. Border of blue and black geometric figures and pink roses form a wreath. The name was given to it by the Larkin catalog #90.

BURMA 71854 MM-22. Geometric border is black and yellow with cadet blue medallions. Oriental birds and flowers. The same pattern as Sheila, except Sheila does not have central bird.

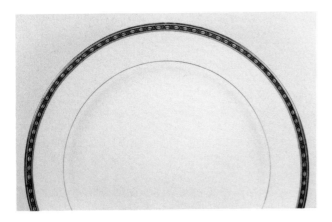

CAMBRIDGE MM-22. Gold edge. Narrow border is geometric with black and green lines and band of yellow and white circles and broken ovals on black ground. Wide cream band to inner gold line.

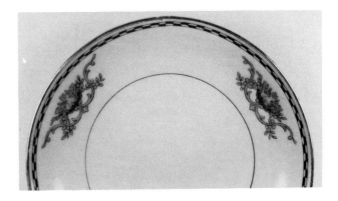

CAMILLA MM-22. Gold edge. Narrow yellow-brown band and then a narrow black and white chevron band. Cream background to inner black line encloses blue-gray scrolls holding pink, rose and green sprays.

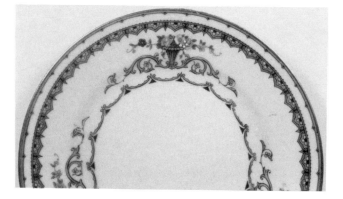

CARLTONIA 78048 MM-22. Gold edge. Double border of yellow-brown and black, pale cream and green. Floral bouquets with overglaze enamel dots in blue and white are arranged in a mustard vase with branching mustard scrolls on the cream background to beige inner scroll, accented with black triangles. A bright pattern. Amorosa has the same pattern number but is not the same design.

CASINO MM-18. Cornflower blue and lemon yellow border in design of scrolls and leaves. Pastel florals below border on a cream background.

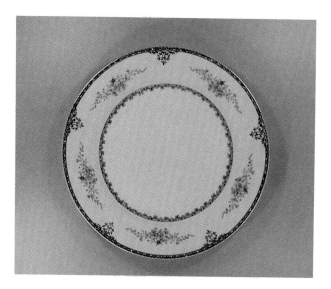

CASTELLA 80463 MM-18, MM-21. Tan, black and white border with heart-shaped motifs dropping into the cream ground. Inner band is black, tan and gray. Pastel flower groups on cream ground.

CELTIC (The) MM-19. Delicate early border. Pale blue reserves holding pink roses are surrounded by yellow scrolls.

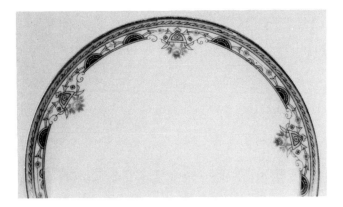

CHANAZURE 61239 MM-22. Gold edge. Narrow border pattern with band of gray blue enclosing a pale ivory leaf chain edged in black, above a broken band of tiny pink flowers enclosed in gray-blue with blue and black half-circles joining wider sprays of pink roses.

CHANDELLA 68478 MM-22. Gray-blue, black and tan intricate border with gold pen line ¾" beneath. Gold edge, all white background.

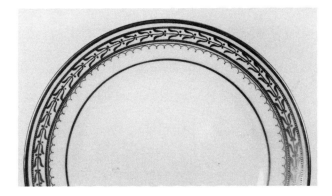

CHANFAIRE MM-19 in magenta. Design is all gold and cream to inner gold line. Center white.

CHANESTA 68454 MM-19. Gold edge. Dark blue and gray-blue border with medallions connected by a black pen line. Cream background above. Same design as Bancroft but colors are different. Pictured is a chop plate.

CHANLAKE 68457 MM-22. Gold edge with black and white verticals forming the border. A one-inch band of blue scrolls on a cream background with pink roses and green leaves connecting ends with a gold pen line below.

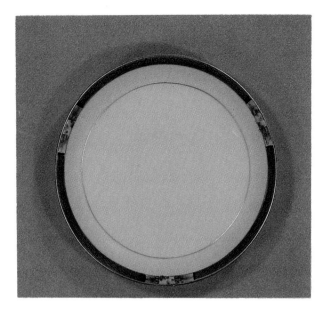

CHANOSSA MM-19. Dark tan border with black geometric design and insets of pink roses with purple foliage on a white ground. Cream background ending in a gold pen line separates the design from the white center.

CHANTARO 61241 MM-22. Yellow and black geometric border, and then an elaborate pattern of yellow and green cameos, scrolls and beading with swags of pink roses and green leaves above the gold pen line separating the design from the white center.

CHANVALE MM-22. A bird pattern. Gold edge, black and yellow geometric rim with insets of red berries, green leaves and stems. Lavender and beige scrolls top pink and yellow plants with green leaves on a white ground. Center design is a pheasant on a rock against a plant. All colors somewhat subdued except for yellow rim.

CHANWAY MM-22. Gold edge, then a wide band with black background. A gold design of flowers and leaves is superimposed on the band in a repeating fashion. Reminiscent of the pattern Goldkin. From the collection of a friend of Judith Bruno.

CHAUMONT (The) MM-22. Has ¼" gold band on an all-white body. This is an older and different pattern than Chaumont 6008, a later pattern not included in this book.

CHELSEA 71432 MM-22. A bird pattern. Gold edge, narrow geometric border in yellow, deep blue and leaf green with insets of tan scrolls enclosing yellow, orange and blue floral clusters. Inner gold line separates cream background from white center on which is centered a colorful scene of pheasants near a lake. Bushes with pink and orange flowers surround the birds.

CLINTONIA MM-18. Border of sea green, burnt sienna and orange-yellow below the gold edge. A wide cream band ends in a line of green bars and yellow circles outlined in brown. Cream band is overlaid with flower sprays in peach, melon and yellow, with green leaves.

CONDORO MM-22. Gold edge. Leaf green and tan scroll border appears on inside edge of our cup sample. Green and tan band below the multicolored floral. The placement of the various decorations appears on our bouillon cup sample, as described, but probably are not the same as on the plates.

CONISTON (The) 58599 MM-22. Gold edge. Wide all-over border is medium blue with three different medallions, two being florals in pink, yellow nd blue, and the third a geometric design in magenta. Gold line below. This pattern may also have an earlier backstamp as some pieces say "Nippon" rather than "Japan."

COPLEY MM-22. Wide dark blue border with shell motifs in black and tan alternate with floral medallions below the gold edge. Body of the china is all white.

CORNWALL 71425 MM-22. Gold edge. Gray-blue, tan, black and pale yellow in border. Gray-blue and tan scrolls in border enclosing pink roses and green leaves. Black line connects the floral motifs.

CORONET MM-22. Has a 5/16" gold band that does not wrap the edge, with a gold pen line immediately below. Balance of plate is all white.

CORTEZ MM-19. This pattern is different from the later Cortez 8752. Gold edge, cadet blue and yellow border edged with black. Gray urn with feathers holding three pink and yellow roses with lavender leaves interrupts the border design. Cream background to black line.

COVENTRY MM-22. A bird pattern with gold edge. Gray-blue, tan and orange-yellow border with insets incorporating black. Oriental flower sprays and butterflies on plate rim in shades of light pink, gray-blue, yellow and tan, with olive green leaves, on a cream ground to gold line. Center of plate has a large pheasant in brick, tan, blue and yellow, a butterfly, and additional flowers.

CRAGMOOR MM-22. Gold edge. A rectangle of soft gray-blue encloses an Alladin lamp of gray and white on a pale yellow ground. A longer rectangle with pale yellow ground has stylized leaves at each end and is centered with a circle of pink roses and green vine. Gold pen line ½" below rectangles.

CRANDON MM-18. Gold edge. A green area with tan scrolls compose the border. Multicolored flowers in a scroll vase against a cream background to the green line encircling the white center.

CRETE (The) MM-22. Gold band with black Greek key design superimposed. The body of the ware is all white. Not the same pattern as Crete MM-10 pictured on page 16.

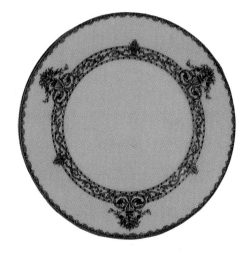

CROYDON 76568 MM-22. Gold edge. A different pattern than the Croydon 5908, which is later. Gray-blue bands with black dots and scallops. Floral design in lavender, yellow and bittersweet with olive green and leaves alternating with goldenrod scroll with black and bittersweet accents. Designs all on cream ground to gold line.

DARBY MM-22. Gold edge. Gray-blue border with touches of lemon yellow. Cream background to wide inner design of gray-blue and olive green scrolls edged in lemon and black bars. Large yellow and black urn holds blue and lavender flowers with a mauve fan alternating.

DATONIA MM-22. Gold edge. Very narrow band in yellow with black scallops and dots. Entire background white. The pictured salad plate has two alternating motifs, one of flowers, leaves, berries and branches — the other is a pheasant with flowers in blue, pink, yellow-orange and tan, red-orange berries, brown branches and green-gray leaves. The pattern is all on a cream ground to the black line encircling the white center. Sample for the book photo furnished by Barbara S. Tompkins.

DAVENTRY 69544 MM-22. Gold edge. Cadet blue and lemon yellow geometric border does not appear in this platter photo, but the dark blue floral band with insets of an urn holding pink roses, on the cream band, does appear on all other pieces. Center of the platter is white.

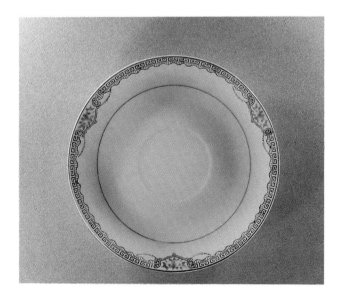

DEERLODGE 69531 MM-19. Gray geometric design border with floral insets and below that the typical ivory band ends in a gold pen line.

DEAUVILLE MM-22. Blue-gray border with floral insets. A gold edge and a gold pen line demarcates the plate rim. White center.

DELHI 71424 MM-22. Gold edge, border of geometric figures in blue and tan with a mustard narrow band below. A ½" cream band broken by an elaborate scroll medallion in blue, filled with flowers and fruits in yellow and orange, with green leaves partly on the cream and extends into a wider white band ending in a gold pen line, completing the design portion of the pattern.

DELMONTE 71426 MM-22. Gold edge. Yellow, black and white band with insets of two kinds of florals followed by a cream section on which are spaced scrolls and a medallion in the shape of a cameo all in black, pink and mustard. This salad plate has three such designs connected by a black line, below which the central portion of the plate is all white.

DORIS 71219 MM-22. Gold edge. Cadet blue and white border with yellow trim below, and with reserves of pink flowers at regular intervals. Gold pen line demarcates the plate rim of this chop plate.

DORRANCE MM-18. Green geometric border with gold edge. Large bouquets of pastel flowers repeated four times on the cream background of the plate rim of this salad plate, and then a row of green scallops encircles the white center, with a smaller bouquet of the same flowers in the center. Mrs. Phyllis Baldwin supplied this piece for the photograph.

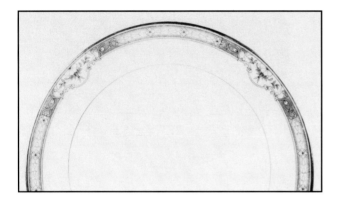

DULUTH MM-22 Gold edge. Narrow border band of lines in hyacinth blue and yellow with cartouches in yellow enclosing tiny bellflowers. Other insets hold a pale pink flower with green leaves. Cream band to tan inner line.

ELLROSE MM-22. Gold edge. Wide band of Alice blue scrolls on a white ground. Two different reserves — one has a brown basket filled with pink roses and blue and yellow daisies — the other a stylized bouquet of the daisies with rust-colored berries added. A blue geometric border below the entire band.

ELMONTE 80754 MM-23. Gold edge and elaborate border in black, lemon yellow, cadet blue and green. Sprays of violet-red, goldenrod and blue flowers with yellow leaves are on cream background. Photograph is of a saucer which does not show the inner design in the same colors as the outer border.

ELYSIAN MM-22. Gold edge. Border of tan and goldenrod with black dots and light blue half-flowers. Wide cream band overlaid with orchid, maroon, peach and cadet blue flowers and olive green leaves, ending in a tan and black inner band. The photo of a cup does not show the bouquet of flowers in the center of a plate.

ERIE MM-22. Gold edge, narrow white space. Black and tan border with interwoven tan leaves and a tan medallion of leaves. Cream band to black line is ½" wide. Center all white.

ESTELLE 83367 MM-18. Gold edge. Leaf green band encloses white flowers with reserves of black and pale yellow scrolls enclosing pastel pink, yellow and lavender flowers. All designs on cream ground to central yellow scroll outlined in black.

FAIRFAX 80461 MM-22. Gold edge. Black and white geometric border interrupted by a yellow flower on a green background. The wide cream background encircling the inner edge of the plate rim has pastel bouquets connected by a pen line that demarcates the white center.

FAIRMONT 80755 MM-18. Gold edge. A delicate pale green border with two different alternating insets. Cream background to center line, white center. Not the same pattern as Fairmont 6102 which is much later and not included in this volume. From Rita Larson's collection.

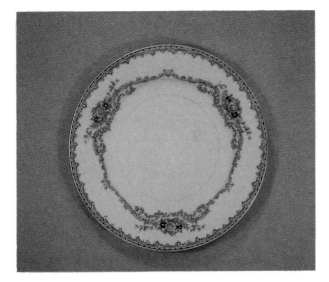

FARLAND 86200 MM-22. Gold edge. Orange-yellow and brown border with similar colored scrolls below and flowers encircling the plate on a cream background. Flowers are rose and blue with pale green leaves. A brown line ends the wide cream band. Center white.

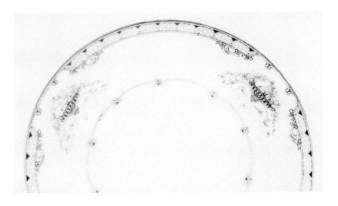

FAVORITA 78057 MM-22. Gold edge. Cornflower blue border has touches of black, white and yellow. Fern green band below, and fern green design at bottom of cream band. Bright multiflorals in black, yellow and brick red urn with green scrolls superimposed on the cream. White center.

FELICIA MM-19. Gold edge. Black, yellow, white and forest green border. Wide cream band ends in dark green inner ring with black outlines. Scrolls on cream band are dark green and the bouquets are pink, blue and yellow with green leaves. White center.

FLEURETTE 76831 MM-22. Gold edge with brown, tan, white and black border. Floral swags on ivory background are a grayed shade of rose, yellow, blue and green. They are connected by a fine black line. Center is white.

FLEURGOLD 77631 MM-19. Elaborate gold designs on cream background to white center.

FLEURY MM-22. Gold edge. The principal motif is an urn filled with fruit and flowers connected by a yellow and black scroll band. Cream background to white center.

FLOREAL 76839 MM-22. Gold edge. Spring green border with white squares outlined in black and an orange-yellow line below. The florals are in delicate pastels on a cream background. Elaborate inner design is spring green and pale green outlined with black and yellow. White center.

FLORENCIA 58591 MM-22. Gold edge. Gray-blue, yellow and dark gray geometric border with gold line immediately below. A 1" band of cream and then a gold pen line.

FLORIAN (BASSETT) MM-21. Raspberry edge with pale blue and green border design. Oriental-type flowers in blue-green, orange, blue and green and a center medallion.

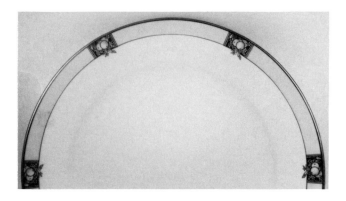

FLORIDA MM-19. Gold edge. A ½" band of golden yellow ending in a black pen line. Insets are black and hold yellow oranges with green leaves. Unforgettable!

FORDYCE MM-22. Gold edge, black line, then a white band. Mustard bars and black dots between medallions of flowers in muted shades of olive, blue, pink and a bitter-sweet alternate with a motif of a vase containing flowers and fruit in the same colors. Cream background to gold pen line, white center. From a saucer.

GOLDENA (The) MM-12, MM-22. Gold band edge ¼" wide on white body. No other decoration. This pattern found labeled "Goldena" alone and often with no name at all. Also found with slightly different widths of gold band but not with a second gold pen line on the plates.

GOLDRAY MM-26. The ⅛" gold edge does not wrap the rim. Gold inner pen line. All white body.

GOTHAM 71437 MM-22. Gold edge. A ⅛" white band bordered at bottom with black pen line, then an ivory band edged with black ovals and dots. Insets of a black and mustard urn filled with fruits and flowers. Below this is a 1" white band ending with a gold pen line.

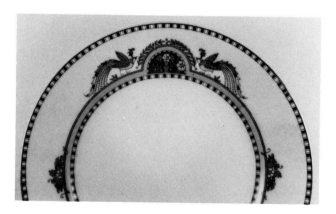

GRANADA 71422 MM-22 A bird pattern. Gold edge. Black and white geometric border. Cream background to black and white center band identical to outer border. Two peacocks face each other with an urn in a half circle between them, and this motif alternates with smaller florals. Colors are muted shades of yellow, brick, olive, black and gray. White center.

GRASMERE 76567 MM-22. Gold edge. Border of clear day blue, black, light brown and white with urns of pink and blue flowers. Cream background to gold line. White center.

HALCYON MM-22. Wide gold etched border, next cream band approximately 1½" wide to gold pen line, white center.

GROSVENOR 68445 MM-22. Gold edge. Narrow yellow-green band, narrow black and white geometric band and a wider cornflower blue band edged in green. Rectangular reserves hold pink roses. A gold pen line about 1" from the edge. All background white.

INWOOD 14763 MM-19 variant. A handpainted Indian Tree pattern. Gold edge, black Greek key pattern in border on ivory band. Rose colored oriental flowers touched with yellow, with green and blue leaves, on a white ground. An elaborate band of black geometrics on cream ground with insets of tan and blue. Central design is a large Indian Tree which appears only on plates and larger pieces but not on the saucers. There is also a pattern named Parnell that is similar to Inwood, except that it is executed on a scalloped blank.

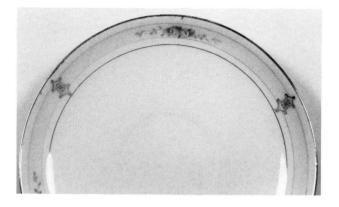

HAVANA MM-19. Gold edge. Delicate border pattern with pale cream band edged in gold. Two designs that are different on cup and saucer. One motif has pink and white roses and yellow-green leaf sprays (touching on cup). The outer is a blue and yellow scroll, one on the cup and a different scroll motif on saucer. The pattern name is on both pieces in the backstamp.

IONA MM-22. Yellow scroll border, with two fruit bouquets opposite each other above a wide orange band separating cream ground from white center. This bread and butter plate is a gift from Barbara Rutter.

IVANHOE 86197 MM-18, MM-36. Gold edge. White rope on bright blue ground edged with bright yellow scrolls and small yellow blossoms with white leaves. Atop the cream background to inner aqua line are multicolored floral sprays. See Mystery 94 for the same border.

JUANITA 76834 MM-22. Black and yellow border with cream area on plate rim to inner circle. Two different flower bouquets alternate on the cream band. White center.

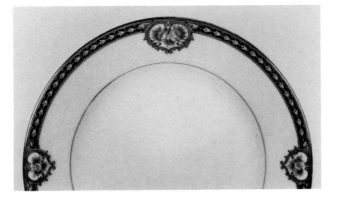

KENOSHA MM-22. Gold edge. Black, yellow and gray-blue border with heart-shaped medallions of gray-blue holding pink roses. Cream background to black line. White center.

KEYBOARD MM-22. Gold edge. Black on white Greek key design with geometric black edging below it. Illustrated in Section IV you will find the pattern named Audrey exactly like Keyboard except that it is on a cream background rather than white.

KNOLLWOOD 68483 MM-22. Yellow and black scalloped border immediately beneath gold edge. Flowering vines and scrolls in leaf green, bittersweet, yellow, tan, black, and gray on a white background encircle plate to inner gold pen line.

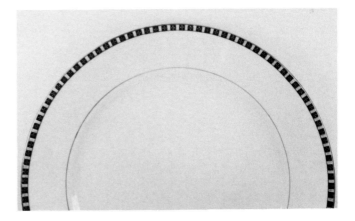

LAFAYETTE 58598 MM-22. Gold edge. Black, tan and white blocks with maroon verticals form a narrow border. Cream background to black pen line. White center.

LA FLEUR 71432 MM-22. Gold edge, wide cream border outlined by narrow geometric bands in black, blue, and yellow on a white ground. Flower baskets in black, blue, and white hold multicolored flowers and green leaves.

LANCASHIRE MM-22. Gold border, mustard band, black line. Floral scroll medallions of green, mustard, and pink, separated by pink flowers with green leaves. A gold pen line demarcates the white center.

LASALLE 69535 MM-22. Narrow pale cream border pattern with tan inner line. Black and yellow rim design, black scroll insets enclosing compotes of yellow roses, fruit, and small blue grapes.

LAUREATE 61235 MM-21, MM-22. Gold edge. Narrow shield-shaped masks in tan, apple green and deep blue. Inner pattern of pink roses with green leaves and swags and scrolls of deep blue and tan. The line connecting the swags of pattern are black, marking off the cream ground from the white center. Do not confuse with Laureate 5651, a later pattern.

LAZARRE MM-22. Sepia edge. Buff and black border design and below that a wide white band decorated with oriental motifs in green, brick, blue, pink and brown, and next a band of buff overlaid with black scrolls and touches of brick and blue. There is a vase of blossoms in the center of the plates.

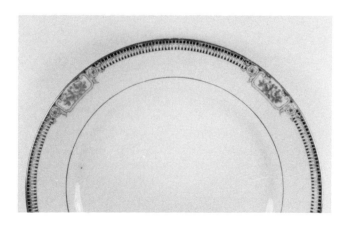

LEROY MM-22. Gold edge. Geometric border of black and white with insets of pink rose and green leaf medallions in a yellow frame. Cream ground to inner line. White center.

LINCOLN 68469 MM-22. Gold edge. Narrow band in jade green and yellow on white and edged with green. Ivory ½" band to black inner line connecting small flower sprays in pink and blue with tiny green leaves under jade scrolls.

LOCARNO MM-22. Gold edge with dark scallops beneath. Cream background to center line is decorated with flower and leaf sprays supported with a green lattice. White center.

MAJESTIC 58596 MM-22. Gold edge. Light blue band design on cream background. Continuous scrolls and swags of flowers in navy blue, rose, light blue and green on cream background. White center. This piece is the lid for the covered round vegetable tureen.

MALVERN 69538 MM-19. Gold edge. Yellow and black border and inner band connecting blue scrolls filled with thistle, grapes, roses and fruit. There is a ¾" black line below first border and a narrower white space before the inner goldenrod border begins. Center white.

MARCISITE 87196 MM-26, MM-34. Gold edge. Elaborate gold border on a cream background to a gold pen line. White center. Entire pattern cream, gold and white.

MARGATE MM-22. Gold edge. Cadet blue bands outline white and yellow diamonds and black triangles. Reserves enclose pink roses with moss green leaves. Cream background to gray line. White center.

MARIANA 76972 MM-22. Gold edge. Bright violet-blue border edged with pale yellow line and black dots and scrolls. Flowers and fruits in bright colors in a gray-blue and white urn (all on cream background) are connected by a geometric band of mustard and black. White center.

MARIGOLD 71436 MM-22. Gold edge. Narrow band of yellow and blue diamonds edged in beige. Wide cream border with groups of pink, yellow and blue flowers over swags of blue and yellow. All outlined in black. White center.

MARILYN 80467 MM-22. Gold edge. Dark sea green border with yellow band beneath. Pink, blue and yellow florals alternate with elaborate green scrolls touched with yellow on the cream background. Another wide band similar to border is green, outlined in yellow, then a cream band to the black center pen line. White center.

MARSEILLES MM-22. Gold edge, tan band. Black vertical lines in border, then a white bellflower border on a light blue ground. Below this a cream wash to the gold pen line. White center.

MAYFAIR MM-22. Gold edge. Gray-yellow geometric design border, then a cream band with swags in a Lincoln drape effect separates the cream from all white center.

MAYVILLE 69541 MM-22. Gold edge, then a light brown and white bellflower border on a black background, with olive green dots between flowers. Gray-blue bands above and below border. A continuous band of gray-blue and black scrolls, swags incorporating small pink roses on a cream background to a light brown line, then the all white center.

Not Pictured:

MAYFLOWER 76582 MM-22. Gold edge. Border is yellow with touches of blue. Strong oriental elaborate flowers in blue and red. Wide inner border. Central motif is repeated flowers.

MERINGO MM-22. Gold edge and inner line separating the cream rim of plate from the white center. This geometric border is made up of diamond-shaped chain effect with insets of a small rose floral within a dull blue scroll design. Other colors used are mustard, tan and green.

MINARET 78049 MM-19. Gold edge. Border of black and yellow stripes. Cream band below encloses turquoise scrolls, the larger design with turquoise and black épergnes, green stalks and leaves and pink and yellow flowers. Inner circle design in black and yellow. White center.

MINERVA 69542 MM-22. Gold edge. Gray-blue and black half flowers in a border of mustard, black and white. Black pen line connects motifs of pink roses and green leaves in a gray-blue and yellow scroll and urn. Cream background to pen line. White center.

MODESTA 69546 MM-22. A bird pattern with violet-blue, black, gray-blue and green-yellow border design. Gold edge. Dark violet-blue medallions edged with yellow alternate with oriental flowers in muted colors on an all white background. Photo is a saucer which does not show central bird motif.

NOT PICTURED:

MONICA MM-22. Gold edge. A twisted rope border in yellow on medium green background with floral medallions dropping into the wide greenish-cream plate rim on which are pink, yellow and blue large sprays. Another ¼" bank in medium green separates white center from border designs. Older and different from Monica 5817.

MODJESKA MM-22. Gold edge, orange-yellow, black and tan border. Black pen line connects brightly colored fruits and flowers in a gray-blue urn. Cream background to black line, white center.

MONTCLARE 58593 MM-21. Gold edge. Border composed of yellow band with blue fork-like geometric design inside. Next, white background with horizontal blue lines up to a yellow pen line. Also, at intervals, are insets of a pink rose against a blue background, this completes border. Body of piece is all white.

MONTEBELLE 80466 MM-22. Gold edge. Border gray-blue, orange-yellow and black, with insets of pastel flowers. Inner border of violet-blue and yellow connects blue urns filled with roses and blue berries touched with enamel. Cream background behind florals. White center. From a pitcher. Pattern arranged differently on plates.

NASHUA MM-19. Gold edge. Black border design with yellow ovals centered by black dots. Cream background to blue and tan scalloped inner line which is interrupted with florals in a tan container. White center.

NAVARRE 69545 MM-22. A bird pattern. Gold edge. Black and mustard border with medallions incorporating olive green leaves and edged in a black scroll. Oriental flowers in light blue, lavender and peach, with olive green leaves are spaced on the plate rim. Two birds with yellow breasts are perched on a flowering branch in center of the plate. All white background.

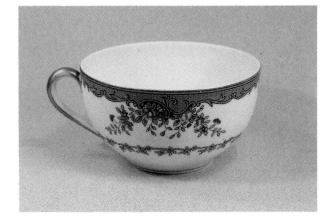

NORDICH 81857 MM-18, MM-22. Gold edge. Border in two shades of green, edged in deep tan. Against this border are two groups of floral sprays in bright colors on a cream background. Inner line design is a garland of tiny pink flowers and pale green leaves on a beige stem. White center.

NORMA MM-18. Mustard band surrounded by brown and with brown scallops below. Gold edge. Floral and scrolls on wide cream background is continuous and in vibrant colors of rose, blue, green, and tan. Tan line demarcates the white center.

ORMONDE 14369 (BASSETT) MM-21. Gold edge. Oxford gray and white border, then a 1" band of rose and light pink roses with pale green leaves on a background of light tan stripes. This band is finished at the bottom with tiny oxford gray darts and diamonds. All on a white background.

OXFORD 85963 MM-22. Gold edge. A row of tiny black scallops, then an orange-yellow border edged with blue scrolls and insets of pink, yellow and blue flowers with olive green leaves and black accents. Smaller flower sprays alternate with insets on a cream background to light brown pen line. White center.

PAISLEY 69543 MM-21, MM-22. Gold edge. Black and white geometric border with insets of bowls of fruit surrounded by khaki-colored fine bands. White 1" band with sprays of oriental flowers down to gold line. The central design is a large pot of fruits and flowers in shades of blue, gray, bittersweet and yellow. The pieces with MM-21 have an extra flower spray to the right of urn.

PARAGON 74083 MM-19. Gold edge. White vertical rods against black background, interrupted with pink rose reserves. A band of cream to the line demarcating the all white center.

PASADENA MM-22. Gold edge. Black and yellow geometric border with mustard scroll insets against a black-dotted gray background. Cream background to inner scroll, which is similar to the border. Groups of bright flowers atop the cream ground. White center. This is an old pattern, different from Pasadena 6311 (not pictured).

PASTELLE MM-18. Gold edge. Black scalloped line, band cream with reserves of scroll enclosing multi-colored flower bouquets, connected by narrow bands of blue with white flowers.

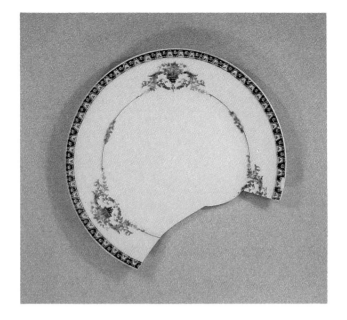

PATRICIAN MM-18. Geometric border in black, tan and white. Tan scrolls surround a black and white vase holding pink roses with swags of flowers and berries connecting each vase motif to a black line separating cream background and white center. Sample furnished by Margo Jenkins.

PEKIN MM-22. Colorful oriental floral pattern with gold edge. Border is cadet blue, yellow and black on white. Bouquet in bright colors is surrounded by smaller sprays of the same flowers, all outlined in black. All white background.

PENDARVIS MM-18, MM-39. Gold edge, narrow band in three shades of green, then large groups of bright floral sprays in pink, blue and yellow with green and gray leaves. The piece pictured is a dinner with an inner design line.

PENELOPE MM-22. Gold edge. Narrow border design in black, dull green, yellow and white. Wider cream border enclosing a different geometric pattern in the same colors, broken by bright floral sprays in pink and blue with green leaves in mustard and black basket vases and mustard scrolls. All lines are black. Not the same as Penelope 4781, a later pattern not pictured.

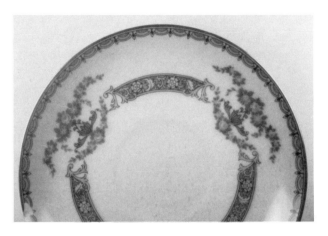

PERDITA 78054 MM-22. Gold edge. Deep blue-green band trimmed at the bottom with yellow circles. Cream background on which are spaced flower groupings in a mustard and black vase. Flowers are dark blue, mustard, maroon and lavender, with touches of bittersweet. Olive green leaves. A black pen line connects the flower sprays and borders the cream background. Entire center is white with a large floral and scroll in the middle, with colors of florals repeated.

PERSEUS 78053 MM-22. Gold edge. Medium blue half-circles with scallops of pale blue and pale yellow below accented with black darts. Pale cream background upon which appear blue and yellow urns filled with pink and blue florals with green leaves and a swag of pink roses below. Floral bouquets are connected with a ½" wide blue band bordered in yellow, with yellow and white flowers within the blue. White center. From a saucer.

PHEASANT MM-22. A bird pattern with oriental look to it. Black edge, orange-yellow and black border design with medallions of pink, bittersweet and light blue flowers with green leaves. A large bird design in center on all white body.

PHOENIX BIRD MM-28. An all-over pattern in bright dark blue with flying phoenix birds and oriental flowers. Similar to Howo. Sometimes called "Flying Turkey."

PREMIER MM-22. Gold edge. Alice blue border design with touches of light yellow-green and lemon yellow continuous scrolls and swags of flowers in navy blue, rose, light blue and green on the cream background. White center. Border is same as Laureate except blue is lighter.

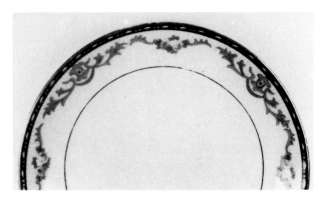

RADCLIFFE MM-22. Gold edge. Narrow border of alternating tiny cadet blue circles and yellow and black ovals against a black ground. Lemon yellow vertical stripes above cadet blue scrolls, with bright pink and white roses, green leaves and swags. Gold inner line. From a saucer.

RAISED GOLD MM-19. See 42200 for pattern description.

REIMS (The) MM-22, MM-18. Gold edge. Gray and tan geometric border, gold pen line. Sample furnished by Barbara Scibetta.

RESILIO 86198 MM-18. Gold edge. Forget-me-not blue and orange-yellow border of scrolls and leaves. Cream background to tan line and on cream are floral sprays in rose, lavender and blue with green leaves. Center is white.

ROCHAMBEAU 61228 MM-22. Gold edge and inner pen line. Narrow band holding three different designs in yellow frames edged in black against a gray-blue background. Larger design is a vase holding two pink roses. Small blue-gray blossoms and gray-green leaves.

ROMANCE 76835 MM-22. Gold edge. Bright blue and yellow border with insets of yellow scrolling against black. Wide cream band enclosing two different muticolored floral groups with mustard scrolls joined by a tan inner line. This pattern has same border as Mystery 27, but the colors in Romance are brighter.

ROMEO 80459 MM-22. Gold edge. Black, blue and bright yellow rings with black dots. Cream band to black line, white center. Cream area adorned with large groups of florals in a vase.

ROMOLA 76840 MM-22. Gold edge. Narrow border of yellow scallops against brick red. On the cream background, below border, are yellow compotes holding fruit and flowers touched with enamel. A multicolor floral wreath separates cream area from white center.

ROSEARA MM-22. Gold edge, parrot green band, then black and white figured band. Cream background with olive green leaves and blue and red-orange flowers, superimposed. Cream ends in a black line and yellow and black scroll motif. Center is white.

ROSEMARY 71629 MM-22. Gold edge, narrow yellow band, then a black and white geometric band. Cream background behind the designs of gray-blue and black urns filled with pastel flowers, encircle plate connected with a black pen line. Center is white.

ROSEDALE MM-17. Formerly listed as Mystery 53 but now identifiable by name. Our sample is a square salad; other pieces may have a different arrangement of large pink roses and fern green leaves. Gold verticals in gold scrolls between the roses. Swags of brilliant florals encircle the plate on a cream background to a tan line and a gold line. A floral group on white ground in center.

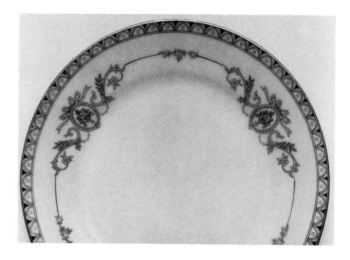

ROSEWOOD 71427 MM-22. An oriental design, gold edge, spruce green and mahogany border and wide inner band enclosing flowers and leaves in the same colors. Flowers in pink, yellow and gray-blue extend upward into plate rim. A large central motif of the same florals. All white background.

SAVONA 68470 MM-22. Gold edge, blue-gray, black and mustard geometric border. Cream background to black pen line that connects mustard, blue-gray and olive cameo-like motifs and also 3 pale pink roses with green leaves. Center of plate is all white.

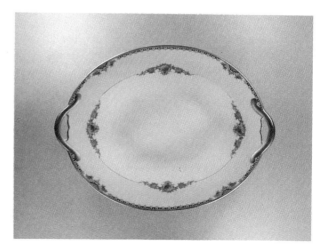

SEDALIA 80553 MM-22. Gold edge. Rich violet-blue bars in border separated by yellow, olive and dark gray designs and a narrow yellow band and scrolls beneath. Cream background to elaborate inner band incorporating the same colors as outer border. Multicolor floral sprays on the cream background. Center all white.

SEVERY 81603 MM-22. Gold edge. Narrow border of yellow, blue and white dots connected by small floral insets. Cream background to black line, which demarcates the cream from the white center and has larger floral groups inset at intervals.

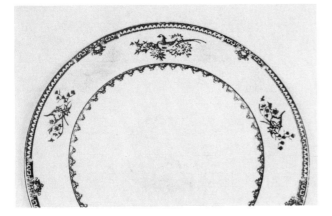

SHEILA 71854 MM-22. This pattern is identical to Burma, also listed in this section. However, Sheila does not have the central bird motif.

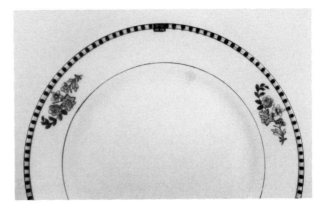

SHERIDAN 69533 MM-22. Gold edge. Narrow band of black verticals on a Delft blue background. Florals are in the oriental manner in purple, blue, yellow, rose and green. A black line demarcates the plate rim. Body of the china is all white. This pattern is not the same as Sheridan 5441, which is not illustrated in this book as it is a later pattern.

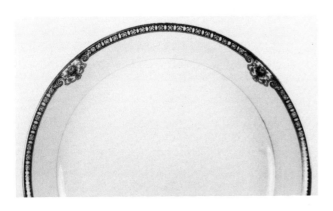

SHIRLEY MM-22. Gold edge. Gray-blue, black and gray-tan border with medallions of peach-colored roses with green leaves in an urn, surrounded by gray-blue scroll. Cream background to black pen line. White center.

SORRENTO 76965 MM-22. Gold edge. Narrow border of fish scales in bright blue, yellow and apple green. Cream background to black inner pen line which is broken by designs of fruit and flowers in orange, yellow and green arranged in an épergne. Vivid colors. A later Noritake pattern, Sorrento 7565, is entirely different and not pictured.

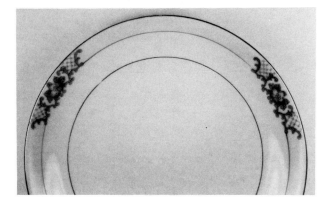

STANLEIGH MM-22. A delicate border with gold edge. Narrow cream band with inserts of gray-blue scrolls enclosing orange fretwork and one magenta and white flower with green leaves. Black line, then white band to inner gold line. Center white.

SUPERBA 76593 MM-22. Gold edge. On the cream background are large vases of flowers with tan scrolls connecting them. A wide orange and tan band separates cream background from white cen-

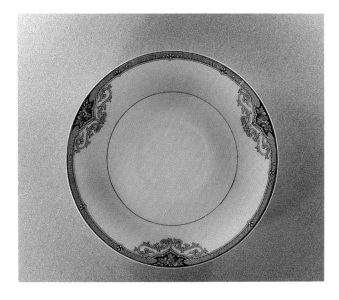

SURREY MM-22. Gold edge. Green border with yellow line, interrupted by fruit and flower bouquets of orange, blue and yellow against black area.

SYLVANIA MM-22. Gold edge. Blue and black outer border then swag of small pink roses and green leaves. Brown scrolls below narrow yellow band with inserts of brown and yellow sconces and winged eagle. Sample furnished by Bev Baker.

SYLVESTA MM-18. Gold edge. Green narrow band, tan-mustard intricate scroll border. Large motifs connected by a black line on the cream background separate the pattern from the white center. Sample furnished by Mr. and Mrs. Mitchell M. Truitt.

THELMA (BASSETT) MM-21. Gold edge. A delicate border with faintly cream background to gray line. Pink roses and green leaves alternate with medallions of yellow cross hatching, blue flowers and lavender scrolls surrounding one pink rose. All body of plate is white.

TOKIO 13714 MM-22. An oriental flower style pattern with sepia edge. Intricate border design in black, pale green and yellow on a faintly gray-tan background. Swags of watercolor shades of pink, blue, green and yellow flowers below border encircle the plate. A pale gray pen line demarcates the plate rim. Small flower group in center. All background is white.

TREE IN THE MEADOW MM-19. Gold edge. Rich autumn sunset colors. Described in the Larkin catalogs as a "scenic" pattern, this pattern has come to be known by collectors as "Tree in the Meadow."

VASONA MM-22. Gold edge. Narrow scroll border in bright yellow and blue, edged in black. Floral groups are pink, blue and tan with green and tan leaves and a tan épergne. Inner line black, center white.

VASSAR 68465 MM-22. Gold edge. Border of aquamarine, black and yellow, with reserves of orchid roses and green leaves. Cream plate rim to gold pen line. White center.

VISALIA 80462 MM-22. Gold edge. Border is a narrow geometric pattern in black and mustard. Floral sprays on the cream background are pink with yellow centers, green foliage and tan and blue scrollwork. Inner design separating the rim pattern from the white center is black, deep blue and mustard. Quite similar to Castella.

WADLEIGH MM-22. Gold edge. Medallions separated by leaves and flowers with inserts of floral design against cream background compose border. Sample furnished by Mrs. W. H. Young.

WASHINGTON MM-22. Border is gold etched band with gold pen line immediately below. All white body.

WELLSDALE MM-22. Gold edge. Green and tan geometric border. Large pink and blue floral on cream background to a scalloped inner band. All white center. Sample furnished by Patricia Pruitt.

WESTMINSTER MM-22. Gold edge. Gray-blue and white dot and oval band. Below that a scrollwork of gray-blue with pale lemon yellow flowers and olive green leaves on a tan background. Balance of plate is all white, with gold pen line at plate rim.

WILDFLEUR MM-22. Gold edge. Cream background to inner geometric design of black and yellow. Bright bouquets of pink, yellow and blue with bright green leaves. A floral design in the same colors on a white center.

WINDSOR 71432, 71433 MM-22. A bird pattern. Gold edge, dark gray and pale yellow border design and inner circle. Cream background on which are spaced florals of pink, yellow, blue and mahogany flowers and berries. White background to gold pen line at base. Not shown on this sample of sugar and lid is a center motif of two pheasants with flowers and foliage. Chelsea also bears number 71432, but is a different pattern.

WINONA MM-22. Gold edge, border composed of two narrow blue bands, which enclose a geometric hexagon figure of white outlined in black. A cream narrow band follows beneath. In addition are insets of fruit (orange) and berries (blue) with green leaves, against a black background. Two blue cornucopiae, filled with yellow, orange and blue fruit, open into the body of a white plate.

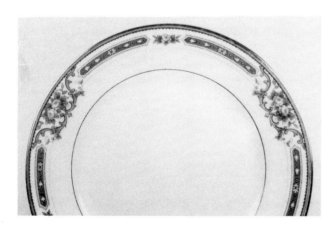

YBRY 76832 MM-22. Gold edge and gold inner pen line at plate rim. Superimposed on cream background are mustard brown scrolls enclosing pink roses, blue and yellow grapes and green leaves connected by blue bands outlined in yellow, plus alternating smaller groups of one pink rose and leaves. White center.

YORK MM-21. Gold edge. Pale aqua and tan scrolls in border. Cream background to tan line with florals in red-orange, tan, cadet blue and pale yellow, with pale sea green leaves. White center.

20056 MM-19. A black, gold and white design with raised gold work. Pictured on the cover of this book.

26979 MM-19. Navy blue and gold border. Cadet blue horns of plenty filled with yellow and red fruits, green leaves and scrolls, separated by two semicircular motifs and between them, a smaller yellow and blue design. All pattern border on a cream background to gold line. Center white. Pattern often found with no identifying pattern number.

42200 MM-19. Large flowers in dark peach and cornflower blue with gold leaves, flowers, buds and scrolls, all accented with heavy gold raised edges. Cream background to gold line, white center. This pattern was called "Raised Gold" in Larkin catalog #109 for 1933.

61229 MM-22. Gold edge, all white background. Large dusty-rose blooms, with yellow centers borne on stems carrying three groups of lavender gray leaves, alternate with butterflies of similar coloring but touched with enamel at wings' edge. This pattern often found with no identifying number.

MYSTERY 5 MM-19 in red. Gold edge. A bright green band to black line. Cream wash to wide yellow band with black pen line surrounding it. Oriental flowers on the cream-colored plate rim in yellow, orange and blue, with olive green leaves.

MYSTERY 9 MM-22. Gold edge. White band to gold line. Design of black medallions alternate with florals in bittersweet, yellow, blue and green, enclosed in gold lines. This is a celery dish.

MYSTERY 13 MM-19. Gold edge. Black, goldenrod and gold design on cream background to a gold pen line. Center white.

MYSTERY 21 MM-19. Gold edge. Border is bittersweet, cadet blue and black. A cream band overlaid with a large floral in rose, orange and bright blue, with big green leaves, ending in a black pen line. White center.

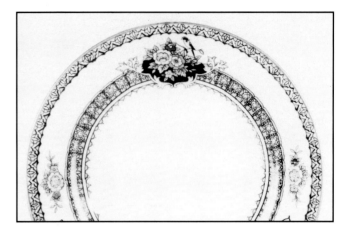

MYSTERY 22 MM-19. Gold edge. Sky blue border incorporates blue forget-me-nots with yellow centers and large green leaves. Below the border, the exterior of the piece is lustered.

MYSTERY 23 MM-19. Gold edge on cream-colored body. Rim and inner geometric designs are white and apple green with heavy black lines. Inserts of blue and yellow birds and floral sprays in bright multicolors against a black ground enclosed in a bright mustard scroll. Similar to Aeolian, but colors are darker.

MYSTERY 29 MM-18, MM-26. Gold edge. Leaf green design in border. Cream background to tan line. A large pink and white open flower and a brick red bud, with large green leaves, the design is on a cream ground. White center.

MYSTERY 31 MM-26. Gold edge. Burnt orange and fern green border. Tiny multicolor florals on cream background to tan line. White center.

MYSTERY 32 MM-19. Gold edge. Orchid band edged in black. Pink roses, green leaves and branches alternate with yellow and green bellflower motif on white background to tan line. Center white.

MYSTERY 35 MM-26. Gold edge. Light orange-yellow border with ivory flowers and bells. Scrolls of lemon yellow encircle plate with pink, blue, yellow and bittersweet flowers intertwined with green leaves. Cream background to yellow inner design. White center.

MYSTERY 38 MM-19. Gold edge. Narrow lemon yellow band, then black on white with yellow design of half circles and vertical lines. Medallions of fruit in red, yellow and blue edged with scrolls. Cream background to dark gray inner pen line, with large floral in bright multicolors superimposed. White center. Sample furnished by Betty Halton.

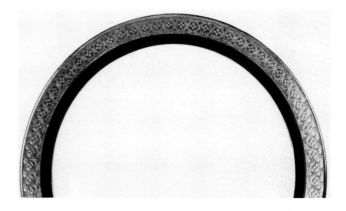

MYSTERY 43 MM-22. Wide gold-etched band with cobalt blue band below, edged with gold pen line separating border from white center.

MYSTERY 47 MM-19. Gold edge. Green narrow border, blue horn-of-plenty.

MYSTERY 64 MM-17, MM-23. Gold edge. Narrow mustard band edged with black pen line. Flower groups atop a mustard scroll are bittersweet, lavender and blue-green with a few leaves of moss green. A ½" mustard and black band is below the florals and then the plate is cream to the black center circle. Interior of plate is white.

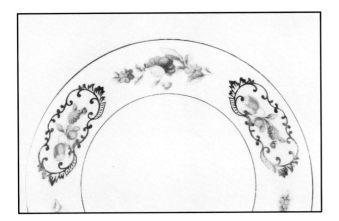

MYSTERY 74 MM-18. Gold edge and gold inner line. Bright Dresden-type floral with gold filigree surrounding alternate flower groups. Very similar to Dresdena, but this pattern has only one gold edge line rather than two.

MYSTERY 75 MM-19. Entire pattern gold, cream and white. Narrow geometric border and below this two gold floral patterns (a different one on front and back of cup). All on a cream background to gold line separating cream from white.

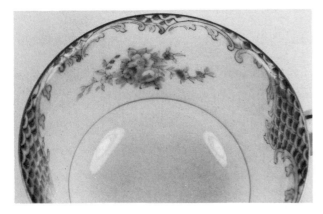

MYSTERY 76 MM-26. Gold edge. Rim design of yellow scrolls outlining bright blue fish scale motif. Wide cream border to inner tan line encloses colorful floral sprays. Hand-decorated. From a cup.

MYSTERY 79 MM-26. Robin's egg blue edge, wide pale yellow border ending in a ¼" band of blue. White center.

MYSTERY 80 MM-19. Gold edge. Yellow and black geometric border, then a pale yellow band enclosing a black compote holding colored fruits and leaves.

MYSTERY 82 MM-20. Gold edge. Hand-painted roses in pink and yellow with leaves in lavender-gray and gray-green. Entire background a patting of pale yellow with orange wash.

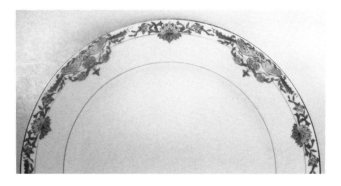

MYSTERY 86 MM-26. Scalloped gold edge with white background, then a wide green border edged at bottom with brown scrolls and gold rays. Central design is a bright multicolored floral bouquet with hyacinth blue shadow foliage.

MYSTERY 91 MM-22. Gold edge. A bird pattern with bright yellow birds with purple tails that alternate with florals in lavender and yellow with green leaves. Cream background to inner gold line. White center.

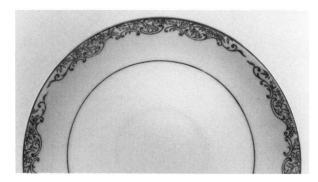

MYSTERY 93 MM-26. A gold, cream and white pattern. The saucer has only the gold filigree at edge with cream background to gold pen line. There are two different designs on the cup, as well as the same border as on saucer.

MYSTERY 95 MM-22. Gold edge. Narrow yellow rim edged with black. The saucer has three floral sprays which alternate atop a cream band. A yellow, scroll-edged design of a red, a pink and blue flower alternates with these floral sprays and appears on the cup pictured. Pen lines are black.

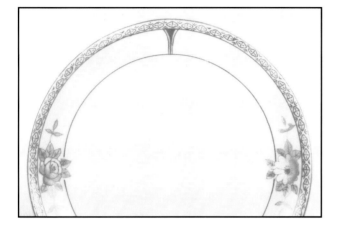

MYSTERY 98 MM-19. Gold edge. Black border on all white background. Black verticals separate floral motifs in lavender-pink and blue with light olive and brown leaves. Brown outlines.

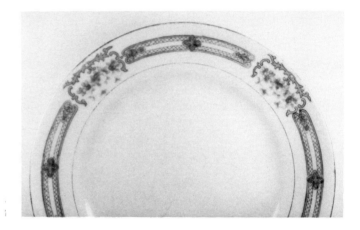

MYSTERY 101 MM-19. Gold edge. Pale gray-blue scrolls outlined in brown alternate with a 3" rectangular motif enclosing a blue and rose stylized flower. The rectangle has pink background, blue and tan crosshatching. The floral under the scroll is rose and blue with pale green foliage.

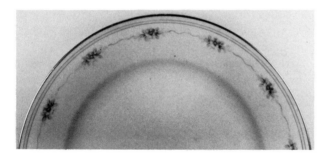

MYSTERY 107 MM-12. Gold edge. Border is cream with two tan pen lines. Below this, single pink open roses with yellow-green and blue-green leaves are separated by a green stem on a white background. A delicate border.

MYSTERY 115 MM-26. Black edge and black pen lines surrounding the leaf and dot circle in rusty red. All on white background.

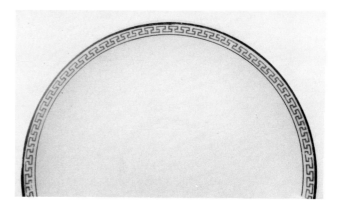

MYSTERY 116 MM-17. Gold edge. Bright green and tan stylized border. Wide cream band to gray and tan geometric line and then a tan band. Below that a ⅓" green band encloses white flowers touched with blue and outlined in black. A large vase and scrolls in green, blue and yellow holds the floral and fruit arrangement in bright colors. Cup has geometric border inside.

MYSTERY 118 MM-22, MM-24. A green Greek key border outlined with gold lines. We have also seen this pattern with a Bavarian mark.

MYSTERY 127 MM-22. Gold edge. Blue bow tops the wreath of lavender roses and green leaves. A ½" band of green leaves connects the wreath designs.

MYSTERY 128 MM-19. Gold edge. Green border mainly geometric with mustard scroll at bottom. Cream band ending in dark line demarcating white center. There is a floral spray of pink flowers and green leaves interrupting the dark line in two places. Sample furnished by Margot Stengel.

MYSTERY 129 MM-19. Mustard scroll border with typical Noritake floral bouquets beneath on a cream background to center scroll which demarcates the white central area. Sample furnished by Elizabeth Harth.

MYSTERY 130 MM-19. Gold edge. Pink rose, attached by a thin black line to a white flower, a delicate pattern.

MYSTERY 131 MM-19. Tan scrolls on orange background with insets of floral swags and larger motif topped with scalloped scroll in green, on a cream background to band demarcating white center.

MYSTERY 132 MM-19. Black border of beading on blue ground with brown band beneath. Large orange and blue florals with brown stems and dark green leaves on a cream ground to black line. All colors are strong. White center.

MYSTERY 135 MM-26. Raised gold roses and scrolls.

MYSTERY 134 MM-19. Strong light green border with white flowers and leaves on pale tan background. Elaborate bouquets of hand-painted Noritake flowers surrounded by pale tan scrolls and then another band of green and tan flowers separate the bouquets. All of this on an ivory ground to brown line demarcating the white center. Sample furnished by Walter Iverson.

MYSTERY 137 MM-26. Gold design and gold flower motif on a cream band composes the border.

MYSTERY 136 MM-26. Gold edge. Green border with fine brown and tan scrolling below. Much more of this scrolling surrounds the plate and forms swags below the handpainted floral groupings. All on a cream ground to a scroll line demarcating the white center.

MYSTERY 138 MM-26. Stylized flowers with green and yellow border of scrolls. Flower bunches appear to grow out of the green line that separates cream background from white center.

MYSTERY 139 MM-19, MM-26. Gold edge. Wide cream band with green scrolls and pale orange design. Motif of multicolored flower bouquets below. Collection of Lee Bennett.

MYSTERY 140 MM-22. Gold edge. Light blue area with yellow-green scrollwork surrounding the plate enclose one pink rose and alternating fleur-de-lis. Also, swags of delicate pink roses compose the border. Inner gold pen line. All white background.

MYSTERY 141 MM-19. Gold edge. This handpainted design by Noritake is like a Charles Field Haviland design.

MYSTERY 185 MM-17. Gold edge. Geometric border of turquoise, black and mustard. Multicolored florals alternate with medallions of scrollwork in same colors. A wide turquoise band ending in a mustard band divides the ivory background from the all-white center. John Lloyd's collection.

MYSTERY 186 MM-17. Gold edge. Green and tan border of rectangles and dots separates ivory background from white center. A large floral of lavender, yellow and blue with green leaves atop the ivory background.

MYSTERY 223 MM-22. Gold edge. All gold design, starting at the border with a narrow diaper band of gold on a cream band. Below are alternating embossed florals and medallions. Inner two pen lines enclose a narrow cream band. The background is white. Sample furnished by Diane Ayers.

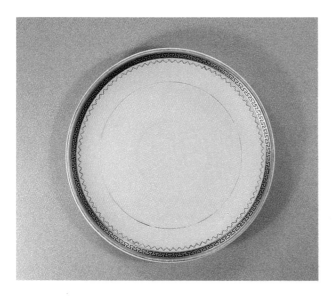

MYSTERY 224 MM-22. Gold edge. Light blue narrow line. Next is a gold band with a keyboard design outlined in black. Below, is a geometric design in black against a white background to a gold pen line. The remaining center is white. Sample furnished by Jerry Richards.

MYSTERY 225 MM-19. Pearl luster center. Green luster edges, separated from center by orange and black cross hatched stripes. A large yellow zinnia and a wine-red zinnia with green leaves are on top of one of the orange strips. Fine gold

MYSTERY 227 MM-18. Gold edge. Elaborate light green border of tan and yellow scrolls surrounding flowers and hatchwork design. Wide cream band overlaid with multicolor floral bouquets in a scroll type vase. Inner light green pen line. White center.

MYSTERY 226 MM-26. Gold edge. Light green background with white flowers enclosed by tan and white scrolls. At intervals, the border design encroaches on the wide cream band. Also on the cream band are multicolored floral groupings at different locations. Then a tan scroll line and white center.

MYSTERY 228 MM-26. Gold edge ⅛" wide. All white.

MYSTERY 230 MM-26. Gold edge. Light green border with white circles, center has green dot, then scrolls of mustard outlined in black. Below is a cream band to an aqua pen line. There are small florals of pink and blue flowers with green leaves. White center.

MYSTERY 231 MM-19. Gold edge. Narrow cream band with alternating wreath and small florals of pink and blue flowers and green leaves. Blue ribbon atop the wreath. White center.

MYSTERY 232 MM-19. Gold edge. Gold geometric design in a narrow band. At intervals attached to this band are ovals of light blue with vertical gold lines. Alternating between a gold raised flower and a gold raised design are two inner gold lines. All white piece. Collection of Joyce Lurtz.

MYSTERY 233 MM-26. Gold edge. Light green-yellow narrow band. Then a white area with green-yellow scalloped line surrounding a broad cream band. Flower groups at intervals encircle the piece in colors of pink and yellow. Leaves are shades of green to a tan pen line. White center.

SECTION III: BACKMARKS MM-29 THROUGH MM-41

MM-29

MM-30

MM-31

MM-32

MM-33

MM-34

MM-29. Circa 1930. This stamp was originally distributed in Australia, circa 1930, then eventually arrived in the United States. First appearance of a patent application for the mold or shape of an actual piece. All in gold.

MM-30. Circa 1930. This stamp had been used for export to the United States, and appears in bright tomato red and yellows. Other delightful backstamps that wear the crown have come in gray-blue and yellow, and sky-blue and yellow. Two noteworthy phrases commonly found are: "U.S. patent application" and "U.S. design and shape patent applied for."

MM-31. Japanese registry 1931. This stamp was reserved for the Noritake acid-etched gold lustreware that was sub-

contracted to decorators specializing in this technique, Pickard in the United States being one among them. The one stamp also appears in green and yellow, bright blue and yellow, pale pink and yellow, and peach and yellow.

MM-32. In 1931 this stamp was issued for Ivory china in pea green and yellow.

MM-33. Note this 1930's stamp with the "tree crest" in place of the Morimura "M". This may have been for export to England.

MM-34. We can only date this all in gold stamp between 1930 and 1933; it is a forerunner of MM-38, which has been dated to 1933.

MM-35

MM-36

MM-37

MM-38

MM-38K

MM-39

MM-40

MM-41

MM-35. This stamp appears in green and yellow. The word "hand painted" is slightly curved above the word "Japan."

MM-36. Very similar to MM-34 and MM-35. Note the tiny bow at the bottom of the wreath.

MM-37. This stamp shows the first use of the "N" alone, to stand for Noritake. In tan and green. This may date after MM-44, a similar stamp that was registered in 1940.

MM-38. 1933 registry. A redesigned "M-in-wreath" stamp, which is the forerunner of the Noritake stamp now in use. Blue-gray wreath, against a mustard-tan ground, with "M" in the center. The bow and background of the rectangle are the same mustard-tan. This is the largest group of pre-World War II patterns we have worked with.

MM-38K. Notice the three sets of numbers in this backmark.

MM-39. Circa 1933. Another redesigned "M-in-scroll." Black outlines and lettering have been used against a blue-green and mustard background. Note there is no bow under the wreath.

MM-40. 1934. A newer Azalea backmark showing five and six digit United States patent numbers — all in red.

MM-41. Circa 1933. This is the same stamp as MM-38, but here with the words "Made in Japan." It comes in the same gray-blue and mustard-tan colors; it also appears all in gold.

Floral bouquet designs in various colors have been incorporated extensively throughout the tableware patterns of Section III.

ABERDALE 3808 MM-38. Gold edge. Scallops of spring green, scrolls tan and goldenrod, a wreath of muticolored flowers completely encircles plate on wide cream band to inner yellow scroll circle. Same border as Mimi, flowers different.

ACACIA 509, 98212 MM-38. Gold edge. Lemon yellow border with scrolls outlined in brown; white flowers and fern green leaves. Cream background to center ring of scrolls in yellow with green leaves. Atop the cream band are urns of pastel flowers dominated by pink roses. Urn and branching scrolls are yellow outlined in brown.

ACTON 4001 MM-38. Red geometric design immediately under gold edge. Tan and brown scrolls separating cartouches of flowers in a vase form an elaborate border on a cream background to the central circle demarcating the white center.

ALCONA 613, 100326 MM-38. Gold edge. Green-yellow geometric border and immediately under this a continuous border of spring green leaves. Multicolored sprays of flowers on a cream background to a tan line.

ALEXIS 3721, 108369 MM-38. Gold edge. Border of forget-me-not blue encloses white leaves, flowers and berries and is touched with tan and light brown scrolls. Floral motifs are multicolored. A cream background to center scrolls of tan.

ALFORD MM-38. Navy blue and yellow border, broken by larger design of blue and rose flowers. Below this are yellow scrolls surrounding a multicolored spray on the cream background to yellow and green scrolls forming an inner band demarcating the white center. Picture from a cream soup underplate.

ALLURE 586, 97902 MM-38. Tan, yellow and white geometric border. Cream background behind large multicolored floral sprays with smaller flower groupings on a white background, alternating. All floral designs edged in a lemon yellow narrow band outlined in tan. More cream background ends at tan scrolls, separating cream from white center.

ALREA MM-38. A gold-edged scalloped blank. A tan area with blue leaves and white flowers enclosed by yellow scrolls compose the border. Below this, large floral sprays are superimposed on the cream background to the elaborate scroll center band. Center is white.

ALTHEA 89492 MM-36. Gold edge, geometric border of black, white and lemon yellow. Large dark turquoise blue motifs surrounded by lemon yellow scrolls, outlined in brown, are separated by flower reserves of two different kinds. Cream background to turquoise line in center.

ALVIN 95649 MM-38. Gold edge. Lemon yellow, green-yellow and tan scrolls with white flowers and sea-green leaves. Very wide cream background and center scrolls of yellow and tan. Bouquets are deep rose, blue, yellow and bittersweet flowers with green leaves.

ARABELLA 503 MM-38, MM-39. Gold edge with border below of green points and gold bells. Light blue medallion centered with a rose. Alternating motif is a yellow basket with branching brown stems and scrolls and filled with flowers. All on the cream background to a brown and yellow center scroll.

ARDSLEY MM-32. Gold edge. Gray-blue, black and yellow border and a wide band in the same colors underneath a vase with branching yellow scrolls. Typical Noritake flowers in vase are touched with enamel. The entire body of this china is Noritake Ivory China. Even though we had only a damaged cup to picture, we felt it was important to include this striking pattern. This is very similar to Mystery 116, but colors are more muted.

ARLENE 95645 MM-38. Gold edge. Border is maize with olive green bands. White leaves touched with olive green and a tiny green-yellow flower. Cream background extends well into center of plate and ends with a tan pen line. Large flower groups topped with maize and olive scrolls alternate with smaller groups on the cream background.

ARNAUD 95654 MM-38. Gold edge. Border of leafy scrolls in aqua, turquoise and blue-green with dotted outline in brown. Mustard scrolls incorporated in typical floral sprays on a cream background to inner scroll circle with touches of aqua.

ARVANA 89483 MM-36. Gold edge. Yellow border with small flowers in tan and blue-green form the outline of the border. Rose, white and dark blue flowers in an orange-yellow vase superimposed on the cream background to a blue-green line. Center is white.

ASHFORD 4026 MM-38. Gold edge. Elaborate tan and yellow-orange border of large leaves and small flowers outlined in brown. Bouquets of multicolored flowers interrupt the border and the entire plate rim is on a cream background to the tan central scroll demarcating the white center.

ATHENA MM-38. Gold edge. Yellow, tan and green scroll forms the outer border. The floral sprays are topped with more yellow, tan and green scrolls and the designs are all on an ivory background to a central green line which divides the white center from the balance of pattern.

BANTRY 86209 MM-31. Gold edge. Alice blue designs bordered by yellow-gold scrolling on cream background to gold line. Large central bouquet of typical Noritake flowers on white background, smaller sprays on plate rim separate blue and yellow motifs. The pattern encircles plate with a large floral bouquet on white center. Sample furnished by Pepper Schmuck.

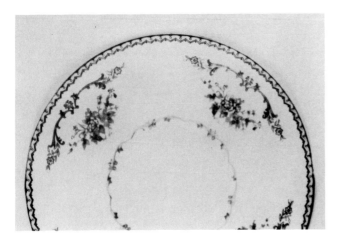

BARTON MM-38. Gold edge. Dark yellow, gray, black and olive green border. A tan scroll tops bouquets of blue, lavender and yellow flowers. Plate rim is cream to a yellow and brown scroll in center. Border is identical to Modjeska.

BASSANO 3720 MM-38. Gold edge. Orange-yellow and tan border of stylized leaves, dots and scallops. An inner wreath of fern green leaves and yellow berries on a wide cream background, ending in center of plate with the same leaf and berry wreath reduced in size.

BAYARD 614 MM-38. Gold edge. Green and tan border. Below that and nearly encircling the dish are typical Noritake florals and scrolls. All on cream background to inner tan scroll that separates cream from white center.

BEAUVAIS MM-31. Gold edge, then an ivory band with tan circles in it. The main border is dark green with white flowers and banded in mustard. A large design with an elegant motif intercepts the dark green sections and just below is a dark green and mustard band. Below this, toward the center, there is one more section of ivory background to the central finishing line demarcating the white center. Sample furnished by Susan Chapin.

BELLODGIA MM-38. Gold edge. White waves on brown, beige and pale green background in border. Two different pastel bouquets on the cream background to inner circle of brown and beige scrolls. Center white. Sample furnished by Dan Meek.

BELVOIR 592 MM-38. Orange-yellow scroll edged with tan. Floral bouquets in multicolors are separated by tan scallops on cream background to tan line. Picture made from saucer. On other pieces, Belvoir has a scalloped scroll where tan line appears near center.

BERENDA 4017 MM-38. Gold edge. Blue border with white flowers and a bit of cross-hatching. Typical Noritake flower groups spaced inside border. Cream background to tan scrolls which separate the cream from all white center.

BLAKELY MM-38. Gold edge. Reddish brown and khaki border and below it, large and smaller bouquets on a cream background. The larger motifs have mustard scroll work beneath them. There is a light brown circle separating the cream background from the white center. Sample furnished by Susan S. Fossum.

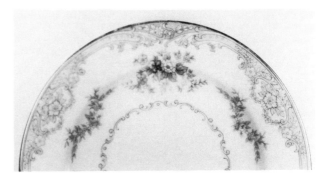

BLUEDAWN 622, 100331 and 4715 MM-38. Gold edge, then a line of upside-down scallops about one inch wide, in blue, encloses small white flowers and sprays and leaves. Floral insets are typical Noritake colors and are on the cream background to a fancy little inner line which separates cream from white center.

BOLERO MM-38. Gold edge. Pale green and light orange-yellow and tan border of scrolls and flowers. Cream background well into the plate ends in yellow and pale blue scrolls. Large bouquets of blue, light pink, yellow and bittersweet flowers with green leaves alternate with smaller sprays of flowers and leaves to nearly encircle plate.

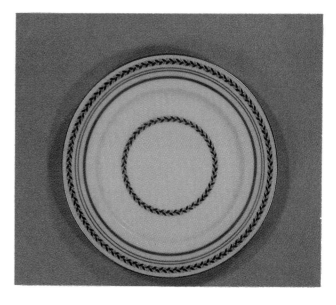

BRANGANE MM-31. Gold edge, scalloped blank. Border design of black and blue-gray scallops, scrolls, dots and fish roe. Floral groupings are orange-red and orange-yellow overglazed flowers with bright green leaves touched with blue, all against the wide cream border. Inner circle of black, white and blue-gray surrounds a central floral pattern. Very bright and bold.

CALIBAN 3733 MM-38. Gold edge. Leaf border in burnt sienna with three gold lines below. Wide cream band ends in inner circle of brown leaves. Entire design brown, cream and gold to white center.

CAMILLIA 3950, 117816, 117508 MM-38. Gold edge, white scrolls and flowers on light brown background edged in orange-yellow scrolls. The cameo design with floral center and swags of flowers flanking it is on a cream background to the light brown and yellow center scroll. The re-issue of this pattern as 4735 bears the mark MM-49.

CANTARA MM-31. Gold edge. Scroll pattern encircles plate in yellow-green against a bright yellow background enclosing white flowers. Large floral groupings in rose, pink, yellow and blue with bright green leaves, are placed on a cream background to inner gold line.

CARDINAL 193, 98829 MM-31. Narrow brick red border with yellow star scroll and flower design on inner edge and tan starburst insets. Alternating large and small pastel floral groups with a few tan scrolls in the cream background to inner scalloped scroll. Center is white. Cardinal was re-issued as 4731 with mark MM-49. Shapes of pieces differ from this original and 4731 has major design inside the cup.

CARMELA 95635 MM-31. Gold edge. Blue and bright yellow border design with a blue lattice area and small blue and yellow flowers. Cream background to gold line has colorful floral sprays. White center. There also was made copy of this pattern marked MM-49 with no pattern name appearing on these pieces.

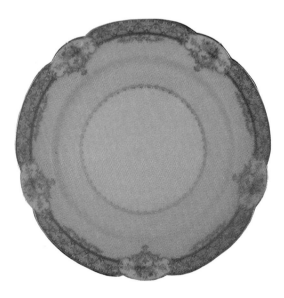

CAVATINA 4011 MM-38. Tan and white scroll band against a brick red background enclosing small tan flowers and leaves. Insets of florals inside a tan scroll. Cream background to inner tan scroll.

CELESTE MM-30. A scalloped blank and the border is mainly a pale aqua or blue green and brown. Spaced between the border area are insets of Noritake florals on a background of white. Entire design executed on an ivory background to the central floral circle which is tan with small dots of the aqua interspersed.

CERULEAN 4726 MM-38. Gold edge. Light blue border trimmed with tan scrolls and interrupting bouquets of blue, orange and ivory flowers.

CHARMAINE MM-32. Gold edge, then black and blue scalloped line. Prominent motifs are a pair of winged lions centered with an épergne of muticolored fruit and flowers and banded at the bottom with a dark area enclosing egg shaped trim in lighter colors.

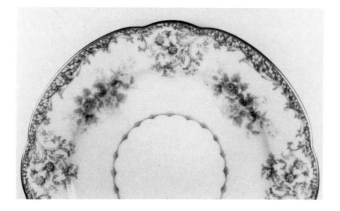

CHARMIS MM-30. Gold edge, scalloped blank. Border of creamy roses on a pale brown background. Below the border, ivory colored scrolls enclose some pink and blue flowers and alternate with larger floral groupings, all on a cream background to central circle of brown scallops. White center.

CHAROMA 98215 MM-38. Gold edge and beneath that a narrow mustard band with alternating white and brown dots, then a scroll area of chartreuse and yellow. Next, typical Noritake florals in two different designs connected and encircling the plate with more yellow scrolls. All this on a cream background to another yellow and pale green band demarcating the white center.

CHERAMY MM-34. Elevated gold border design. Entire pattern is gold, ivory and white.

CHINEBLUE 76842 MM-31. Gold edge, orange-yellow and brown border. Wide cream background to ¼" gold band edged with black pen line. Within the cream are large black and yellow containers filled with multicolored fruits, flowers and leaves, alternating with baskets in pale blue reserves filled with black and white scrolls and flowers and edged in lemon yellow. The pattern is predominantly blue.

CLAIRE 657, 103007 MM-38. Gold edge. Blue-gray and tan border with accents of burnt sienna. Cream background to gold line with multicolored medallion of flowers in the white center. Different from 5902, a later pattern.

CLAUDIA 583 MM-38. Gold edge. Leaf-green and tan border. Below edge, on the cream background, multicolored bouquets and tan and green scrolls form an almost continuous band around the plate with insets of bright colored Noritake florals. Center scroll work is tan and green.

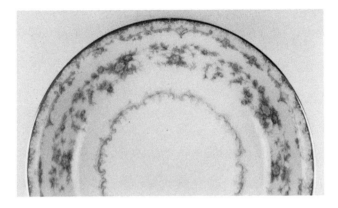

CLEONE MM-38. Gold edge, then a yellow line, green and tan scrolls compose border, and on a cream background, multicolored flower bouquets topped with yellow scrolls encircle the plate. A green line separated cream background from white center. Sample furnished by Mrs. Donna Courtwright.

COLUMBINE 3803 MM-39. This pattern often found with no name or number. Gold edge, narrow tan and apple green border with red accent dart. Another very narrow band of deep cream edging a row of apple green scrolls and tiny flowers. Pale ivory border, which encloses sprays of small, multicolored blossoms, circles the plate. Inner scroll-work is cream and apple-green. Center white.

CORINTHIA 87198 MM-36. Gold edge. Scrolls in deep yellow and white touched with pale yellow on a blue background. Insets edged in green enclose tiny flowers in aqua vases.

COYPEL 3732, 108374 MM-38. Gold edge. Tan and maize border design inset with forget-me-not blue cameos enclosing multicolored floral and surrounded by lemon-yellow and maize scrolls. Alternating with the cameos are flower sprays and swags of yellow encircling the plate. Cream background to yellow and maize center scrolls.

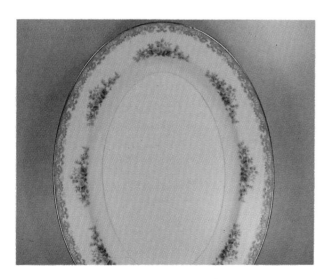

CYNTHIA 655 MM-38. Gold edge. A wide tan leaf border interrupted by colored flowers. An elaborate central scroll of leaves and flowers ends the cream background at white center.

DELROSA MM-31. Gold edge. Narrow band of pea green and a green scroll edge below. Pale cream border to black inner line holds two different alternating multicolored floral groups. The larger spray incorporates mustard and green stylized leaves and flowers on each side. From a saucer. The cup has a wide border of green and mustard below the flower spray in a geometric design.

DELTA MM-36. Border aquamarine and yellow scrolls. Multicolored floral bouquets dominated by a large pink rose almost encircle plate on the cream background to aqua line.

DIANA MM-38. Gold edge. Narrow yellow-green border. Two different pastel floral groups, the larger group topped with scrolls on cream background to brown inner line. Border is the same as Milford 89486.

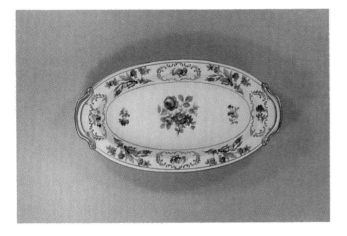

DRESALDA 3849 MM-38. Dresden-type design on white background. Gold edge, lines and reserves. All-over florals in bright colors. Large central flower motif. Another Dresalda 4727 is nearly identical.

DRESDENA MM-31. Gold edge and pen line. All white background with vivid Dresden-type florals alternate with more florals in reserves of fancy gold scrollwork. A large motif of flowers in center. This is a different pattern from Dresdena 6518. See Mystery 74 for a pattern nearly like this one.

DURER 3725 MM-38. Gold edge. The ½" band of white scrollwork is against a pumpkin-colored background. Cream border inside this has groups of green narrow-leafed sprays enclosing a small épergne with three tiny roses in orange, white and pink. Inner scroll motif is pumpkin colored.

ELAINE 89484 MM-36. Gold edge. Black and white border design scalloped and with tan scallops below this. Flowers in rose, blue, bittersweet, yellow and maroon, with green leaves on the cream background to gold line. This piece is a platter.

ELNORA MM-38. Gold edge. Orange area with yellow scrolls compose border. Large floral bouquets of pink, yellow and purple flowers, interrupted by yellow scrollwork connecting the florals, are on a cream background to scrolls which demarcate the white center. This cup appears to be on the scalloped blank.

ELTOVAR 83377 MM-31. Sea green border, orange-yellow and tan scrolls. Carnation pink, yellow and blue flowers in a scroll base on the cream background to a sea-green inner circle of fancy scallops. White center.

ELVIRA 608, 98835 MM-38. Mustard-tan border of scrolls and fish roe under gold edge. Wide cream band with colorful floral sprays encircles plate atop the cream background. Scalloped inner circle separates cream from white center.

EMBASSY MM-39. Fern green border with goldenrod scrolls below the gold edge. Cream background to black center ring with flowers in red, orange, violet and blue, with leaves in various shades of green. This piece is a coupe salad or cream soup underplate.

ESMOND MM-31. Gold edge. Narrow green and yellow-gold scroll with orange sunburst. Border is cream with floral sprays in full color. Inner line is made up of alternating green and yellow scrolls.

EUREKA 502 MM-38. Olive green, tan and black border under a gold edge. Large orange-yellow scrolls surround rose, blue and yellow flowers with green leaves and a garland connects the larger scroll motifs encircling the plate. Design is on a cream background down to the center scroll of green and yellow. This piece is a cream soup underplate. This pattern has the same Japan number as Clayton, but Clayton is not as old and entirely different. Mistakes in labels sometimes occurred during the transitional period when Clayton was manufactured.

FABIAN 684 MM-38. Gold edge. Light mustard border with white flowers and banding edged in brown. A continuous floral design in multicolors encircles this pattern to the light brown circle demarcating the white center. Sample from Lois Johnson's collection.

FARNEY 610 MM-38. Gold edge. Beige border with continuous floral on cream background to central scroll. Sample from the collection of Diane Ayers.

FAUSTINA MM-36. Gold edge. Bright turquoise blue border incorporates light tan and white flowers and leaves. Tan scallops edge the border. Cream background to blue-green line carries muticolored florals and the center is white. Sample furnished by Sharon Snoke.

FIESTA MM-38. Gold edge, a handsome pattern with border of maize and red-orange scrolls and dots and below that, on cream background, bright florals connected by an elaborate scroll pattern in yellow completely encircles the plate. This is the same decal as in Charoma, but the colors are different.

FLORAMAY MM-38. Gold edge. Rim pattern of yellow and mustard scrolls against gray-blue patches and yellow patches with tiny yellow flowers and green leaves. Inner design, on cream background to center scrollwork, has multicolored floral sprays incorporating a large yellow scroll.

FLOROLA 83374 MM-31. Green and yellow-green border bands, and on a cream background and encircling plate, are two different floral groups, the larger grouping incorporating yellow scrolls edged in brown. The inner design, demarcating the white center, is another circle of dark green with green dots on a yellow-green background.

FONDALE 605 MM-38. Gold edge, a border of cardinal red bars and dots and below this, bright floral groups surrounded by yellow scrolls and connected by a continuous band of yellow and pale green bellflowers. All on a cream background to central band of yellow scrolls and pale green darts. White center. Sample furnished by Diane Ziet.

GALAVAN 97894 MM-34. Gold border and entire design is gold on a cream background to a white center.

GASTONIA 98827 MM-29. Gold edge. A molded, scalloped blank. Entire pattern is gold on a cream background to gold inner line. Center white.

GARLAND D167, 95633 MM-34. Gold border. Pattern entirely gold on cream background except for white center. This pattern has a few touches of raised gold.

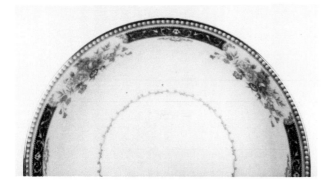

GELEE 3723 MM-38. Gold edge. Border of beige dots and below this, mustard and white scrolls on an oxblood background. Inserts are muticolored flowers. A wide cream band to the inner scroll outlining the white center.

GEORGIANA MM-34. An elaborate gold design on a cream background to central scroll. White center. Square salad plate.

GIRARDO 86205 MM-31. Gold edge. Wide borders of blue-green half circles and medallions, edged with tan scallops. Below this, on a wide ivory background, are large containers of flowers and leaves. Pattern has a brownish cast. Sample furnished by Lynda Ireland.

GLENDALE 5038 MM-38. Gold edge, inserts of tan scrolls and multicolored flower bouquets with a bit of red background. The connecting bands in border are composed of red and pink flowers and tan scrolls. Below this, a wide cream background leads to the white center which is banded with a tan scroll line. Sample is a salad plate.

GLENDOLA MM-38. Gold edge. A multi-scrolled pattern in three shades of green with bright flowers in pink, orange, blue and deep yellow against a wide pale ivory background. Center is white, bounded by more scrollwork in green and yellow.

GLENMORE MM-34. Gold edge, geometric border with elaborate motif in gold on the cream background to gold line demarcating center of white. This a bread/butter plate.

GLORIA 95641 MM-36. Gold edge. Blue-green and goldenrod scrolls. Border with touches of dark brown and small white half flowers. Atop the cream background to green line are bright multi-florals with yellow scrolls beneath alternating sprays. Different from Gloria 6526, a later pattern not pictured in this book.

GOLDCONDA MM-31. Gold edge, scalloped blank. White bellflowers and circles in border accented with tan on a mint green background. A darker green scallop and dot motif above the wreath of pink, yellow, and blue large flowers that encircles this demitasse saucer. Cream background to green line. White center.

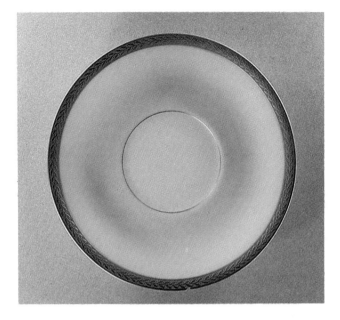

GOLDCREST 470 MM-34. Etched border of gold leaves, then a cream area to inner gold line. White center. Sample furnished by Mrs. Frank Tavaszi.

GOLDENROSE 3981 MM-34. Gold edge. Brick red border overlaid with a gold design. Gold roses and swags in a red vase. Cream background to center gold line. This is a dinner plate.

GOLDINTHIA 87195 MM-34. A wide gold design border over cream background to inner gold line. White center. Sample pictured is a berry bowl.

GOLDKIN 4985 MM-38. A wide gold border with overlay of black flowers and feathers. Cream background to gold line demarcating the white center. A salad plate.

GOLDREAM 469 MM-34. Narrow gold etched laurel leaf band, inner gold line. See Goldcrest 470 for a similar pattern.

GOLDLUSTRA MM-29. Scalloped blank. An elaborate gold design border interrupted by a black and gold medallion. Cream back-ground to gold center ring separating it from the white center. Sample furnished by Margaret T. Thompson.

GRAMATAN 587 MM-38. Gold edge. Lemon yellow and light green border of scrolls, flowers and ribbons. Cream background to tan line with multicolored bouquets superimposed. This pattern nearly identical to Mystery 11 which has slightly different florals.

GRANDEUR 3870, 112930 MM-38. Yellow scrolls touched with gray-blue. This pattern is on a gold edged, scalloped blank has an overall pastel effect.

HARMONY 3906, 117811 MM-38. Gold edge. Narrow band of white and beige scrolls against a burgundy background. Inserted in this band are small groups of pink and yellow flowers with green leaves. Cream background to white and beige inner scroll line.

HAWTHORNE 4914 MM-38. Gold edge, tan keyboard design. All white piece with oriental florals of purple branches and orange, yellow, and olive green flowers. A wide inner band, oriental in design. Center motif of pheasant and a repeated floral as mentioned previously.

HERMIONE 652 MM-38. Gold edge. A scalloped yellow area and then blue scallops below with interruptions of yellow scrolls. Below this, on a cream background and almost encircling the plate, are typical Noritake florals in multicolors, ending at center, with a circle of scrolls demarcating white center. Sample furnished by Mrs. Lila Lawson and Merlanne Smith.

HOLBEIN MM-38. Gold edge and wide tan border of Greek key figures. Below this, an encircling ring of corn leaves and pink flowers on a cream background to a simple scroll line and the white center. Sample submitted by Betty Jean Schneider.

HORTENSE MM-31. Gold edge on scalloped blank. Leaf green and goldenrod border. Florals on cream background are multicolored and the green leaves are touched with enamel. Inner wreath of leaves is in two shades of green. White center.

HYANNIS 3642 MM-38. Gold edge, green band outlined in beige geometrics. Floral pattern has deep rose, blue, lavender and pale yellow flowers with apple green foliage. A wide ivory band to the beige inner line. Photo is a creamer. Pattern on place pieces has a different arrangement.

IDALIA MM-38. Gold edged scalloped blank. Pattern is of yellow scrolls and white flowers against a red border. Grouping of multicolored flowers on an ivory background to the central ring of scrolls demarcating the center.

IRENE MM-31. Lemon yellow with green border on a gold edged scalloped blank. Bouquets of pastel various-colored flowers, some touched with enamel, on a cream background to the central scroll in same colors as the border. Piece pictured is a cream soup underplate.

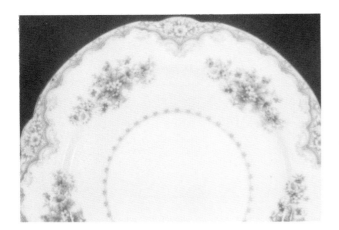

IRIS MM-30. Gold edge, beige and yellow floral border. Ivory background to scalloped scrollwork in center of plate. Delicate floral sprays of green, yellow, blue and red.

JACQUIN 94549 MM-31. Gold edge. Green band with white flowers and leaves and yellow scrolls edged in brown. Cream border holding multicolored floral sprays. Green inner line. Border identical to Jasmine.

JANICE MM-31. Sea green, white and pale yellow-orange border of scrolls and flowers with similar scrolls beneath the floral motif. These florals are rose, yellow and blue with green and aqua leaves. Background is cream down to the center design in aqua and yellow. Pattern executed on a gold edged, scalloped blank.

JASMINE 585 MM-38. Gold edge, leaf green band with white flowers and leaves and yellow and mustard scrolls. Floral sprays on the cream plate rim are white and pink roses and smaller yellow, orange and pink blossoms. Green and pale blue-gray foliage. Inner circle is of small leaves, pale yellow scrolls and tiny white blossoms. The pattern Jacquin 94549 with the backstamp MM-31 has identical border to Jasmine.

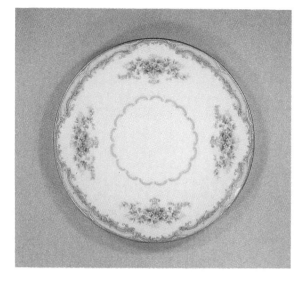

JOAN 584 MM-38. Gold edge, blue-green and pale orange-yellow border with some tan outlines. Cream background to yellow scallops in center. Florals are yellow, pink, blue and green. Center is white. This pattern was also made with no name or number on pieces.

JOLIET MM-36. White and tan scrolls in green border, interrupted by yellow-tan scrolls half surrounding a flower bouquet. A green line, rather than scrolls, demarcates white center. Sample furnished by Deanne Brooks.

JUNO 716 MM-38. Gold edge. Pale blue shading into forget-me-not blue border edged with light tan scallops. A ½" band of cream, then a wreath of tan and gray-tan designs interrupted by flower groupings of pink roses and small blue flowers, all with green leaves. More cream background to center scrolls of blue and tan. White center.

KELVIN 3905 MM-38. Geometric tan border with touches of white. Scroll bouquets attached to border and leaf fern with yellow bow in the middle alternating around plate on a cream background to center ring of scrolls demarcating white center. Sample from Mary Blair's collection.

LADURA MM-31. Gold edge. Brilliant cornflower blue enameled scrolls with a few tan scrolls. The flowers are pink, rose, blue, yellow and orange on a cream background to blue line. White center.

KENWOOD 89482 MM-31. A scalloped blank. Gold lace band with triangular shape medallions in black and gold dropping into plate rim and touching the gold center line. Alternating florals are gold roses and foliage. All pattern is in a cream background to white center.

LANARE 89485 MM-36. Gold edge. Aquamarine border incorporating white leaves and tan and white medallion touched with black. Cream background to aqua line with groupings of typical Noritake flowers atop the cream.

LARAMIE 3754 MM-38. Gold edge. Mustard border. Wide cream band with pink, yellow, orange and blue florals alternating with same color scrolls to a mustard inner scroll line. White center. Picture furnished by Mrs. K. Wildfong.

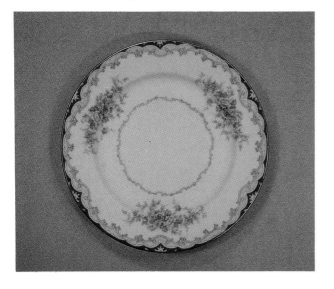

LARES MM-38. Gold edge. Bittersweet, lemon yellow and tan border and scrolls. Cream background overlaid with pastel bouquets. Center scrollwork is yellow to white center. This pattern has the same border as Oradell.

NOT PICTURED:

LARUE MM-38. Scalloped gold edge. Light tan and green areas divided by a line of white circles follow a scallop flow enclosed by tan scrolls on a wide cream band. Multicolored florals at intervals to a light green pen line. White center. Not the same as Larue 6913.

LAURETTE 5047 MM-38. Gold edge, wreath of white and gray flowers, touch of yellow in center, with green leaves, encircle saucer.

LAUSANNE MM-31. Blue, white flower and yellow scroll border. Bird and flower motifs on a cream background are banded at white center with an elaborate wreath of more designs in the same color. Collection of Margot Stengel. Pictured from a soup bowl.

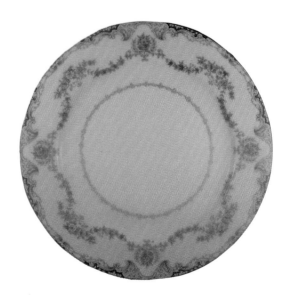

LEONA MM-38. Gold edge. Orange, yellow and tan border with scrolls over multicolored florals. Cream background to yellow inner circle of scrolls. White center.

LILAC 3914 MM-38. Tan scrolls with touches of reddish brown form the border. Muticolored swags and cameo-like designs on the cream background completely encircle the salad plate.

LINDEN 525, 98217 MM-38. Chinese red border with yellow scrolls and leaf fronds on a white background. Cream background to inner band of yellow scrolls. Floral sprays are pink, yellow and purple with green and blue-green leaves.

LISMORE 98836, 609 MM-38. Yellow scrolls and geometric design with red darts compose border. Noritake floral sprays on a cream background to center scroll surrounding a white center.

LORINA MM-38, MM-39. Geometric border like Modjeska of tan, brown and black. Large florals on cream background to scallops. White center. Sample furnished by Karen Franklin.

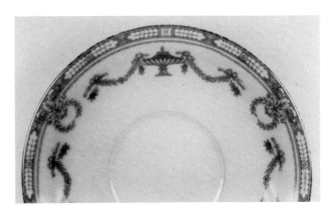

LORENTO 3852 MM-38. Gold edge. Border pea green and deep mustard. Cream background to pale beige inner line encloses groups of lamps, leafy swags with bows and wreaths. From a saucer.

LOYALO 98214 MM-38. Gold edge. An elaborate border in tan and yellows with some gray. Below that are the typical Noritake florals in multicolors connected by an encircling wreath of flowers and leaves. All on cream background to white center which is bound by a smaller ring of scrollwork.

LURAY 95638 MM-36. Gold edge. Bright aqua border edged with mustard and yellow scroll. Flowers are pink, yellow and blue with apple green leaves on a cream background to inner aqua line. White center. Pictured is a square salad plate.

LURLINE 4007 MM-38. Turquoise blue border encloses white leaves and alternates with reserves of multicolored flowers in a tan vase. Scrolls in tan beneath the entire border. Cream background to tan scrolls near white center. Pictured, a soup bowl.

LUXORIA 91602 MM-30. Gold scalloped edge. Intricate border, primarily aquamarine with leaf green scrolls. Pastel floral bouquets, with some flowers touched with enamel, are on cream background to central green scrolls. White center. Cereal bowl pictured.

LYNBROOK 3903 MM-38. Gold edge. Row of white balls on green background above and below light green band with white scrolls. Multicolor floral reserves outlined in tan with white scrolls. Next, a wide cream band to tan pen line. White center.

LYNROSE MM-38. A powder blue border like Juno. The florals nearly encircle the saucer with a tan and blue design below. The cup and saucer from the collection of Margot Stengel.

MADERA 5106 MM-38. Gold edge. Large green leaves and small purple flowers and buds form a wreath-like border. All white background.

MAGNOLIA 3918 MM-38. Gold edge, fern green border of leaves and dots above mustard and yellow scrolls and medallions. Cream background to central scroll motif, and atop the cream band are swags of pastel flowers and scrolls. White center. Sample from Diane Ayers collection.

NOT PICTURED:

MALIBU 3700 MM-38. Gold edge. Cream band to a tan line, white area containing a wreath of olive green leaves and dark red berries to a tan line. Below a wider cream band to a gold pen line. White center.

MARCIA 3855 MM-38. Gold edge. White florals in an exquisite tan and yellow border. Below a medallion with pink roses at the center and a cartouche containing tan and yellow scrolls alternate around the plate, all on a wide cream band. Inner line with green circles to a white center.

MARCOLA MM-31. Gold edge. Light green scallops surround the border. Below is wide cream band of intricate scrollwork in light blue, green and yellow, muticolored flowers and gray leaves also are incorporated into the design. Then a green pen line to a white center.

MARIE MM-31. Gold edge. Gold circle design on cream border. Large cranberry band bordered by a gold lace on cream background to a gold pen line. White center.

MARCELL 86199 MM-36. Gold edge, black scallops on tan, sea green and white band edged with green-yellow stripe and scrolls. Pastel florals atop yellow scrolls are connected by a black pen line. Plate rim is cream, white center. Pictured is a berry/fruit bowl.

MARGO MM-34. Wide etched gold band, cream background to gold pen line. Center is white. Entire pattern is cream, gold and white. Photo of a square salad plate.

MARLBORO MM-31. Gold edge and a design of long bright green scallops with insets of light of light brown. Below this border are light brown sprays of flowers on a cream background to a wide gold inner circle. Center white. Sample from the collection of Kathleen R. Baron.

MARLENE 95642 MM-36. Gold edge. Pale yellow-green band with apple green striping and yellow scroll edge. Pale cream band to aqua-green line. Floral motifs are topped with yellow and green scrolls and are connected by pale beige leaf garlands to encircle plate. White center.

MAYFIELD 7280 MM-34. An urn of gold flowers with scrolls below and an intricate gold scroll border on a cream background. All the pattern is gold, cream and white.

MEDEAN 712 MM-38. Gold edge. Border design of white dots, white scrolls on tan and maize background. Tiny white flowers with pale green-yellow leaves are below the scrolls. The continuous floral border is in pastel colors on a cream background to yellow scroll. Center white. From a creamer. Pattern probably arranged differently on plates.

MEDUSA MM-34. Gold edge, white band with three gold lines, in addition to edge, compose border. Cream background to inner gold circle. Sample furnished by Harriet Grace Fryer Hauser.

MELROSE 370 MM-38. Gold edge. Elaborate tan and yellow scrollwork surrounds pastel bouquets and encircles plate. Cream background to tan center line. White center. From a saucer.

MERLIN 108380 MM-34. Black leaves outlined in gold make up border. Cream background to central gold ring.

MIGNON MM-30. Scalloped blank with gold edge. Entire border in light and dark shades of gray-tan. Delicate oriental type florals in watercolor shades on tan and dark brown branches. Bittersweet berries are touched with enamel. All white background. Do not confuse with Mignon 6652, a later and different pattern, not pictured in this book.

MILFORD 89486 MM-31. Gold edge, orange-yellow and olive green border with medallions of mustard, touched with black and intertwined with pink and yellow flowers. Fan-shaped black basket holds more flowers and branching mustard scrolls, that alternate with the design hanging from border. Cream background to gold center line surrounding white center. Do not confuse with Milford 2227, a later pattern entirely different and not included in this volume. Sample from the collection of Amy Monsen.

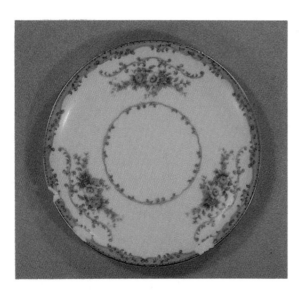

MIMI 98141 MM-38. Gold edge, pale blue-green scallops and below them, tan and goldenrod scrolls. Flowers on cream background are rose, yellow and blue. Yellow scrollwork separates cream background from white center. The edge border is identical to Aberdale, pictured, but florals are different. Sample furnished by Sandy Arnett.

MIRABELLE 3843, 114075 MM-38. Gold edge. Dark and light gray beige border of flowers and leaves. Superimposed on cream background to inner tan scroll are rose, blue and yellow florals in an urn fashioned of yellow scrolls. Motifs encircle plate with connecting swags. White center. A salad plate pictured.

MOSELLE 723 MM-38. Gold edge. Narrow scroll vine band in white on mustard, narrow yellow-gold band, then a row of beading. Wide cream border to inner scroll line enclosing wreaths of flowers in magenta, aqua, deep blue and yellow with leaf fronds in yellow, beige and three different shades of green.

MURIEL 611, 98838, MM-38. Gold edge, mustard narrow band. Light green background, white outlines and then a mustard band enclosed by white circles. Below white area are mustard half circle designs. Next, wide cream band with multicolored florals above yellow leaf scroll. Yellow scallops separated by mustard dots. White center.

MUSETTA 3702 MM-38. Gold edge. Wide cream band with green leaves in upper portion and Greek key design below that. White center. Pictured is a 2-handled cream soup.

NADINE 8035 MM-38. An elaborate gold, cream and white pattern.

NANAROSA 682 (repeated as 4902 in 1953) MM-38, MM-49. Gold edge. Scrollwork is mustard with bright yellow-green leaves and background. Wide cream border with floral groups in pink, yellow, blue and orange and leaves in green, gray and beige. Scroll separates cream border from white center. Often found with MM-49 backmark and no name on the piece. Shapes vary.

NANETTE 683 MM-38. Gold edge. Narrow border in mustard of scrolls and fish roe. Wide cream band with two groups of floral and scroll motif in bright colors and green leaves. Border on this plate is identical to Elvira, pictured, but florals are different.

NERRISA 673, 103009 MM-38. Gold edge, shades of dark and light tan and ivory floral border touched with enamel. Thin white line, then inner cream band enclosed with gold pen lines. The remainder of the piece is white.

NAOMI 674 MM-38. White flowers with yellow centers on forget-me-not blue background edged below in yellow scrolls. Pastel floral sprays on cream background to inner yellow scrolls. White center. 4901, made a little later, has slightly different center scrolls and shapes may vary from 674.

OLYMPIA 680 MM-38. Gold edge. Tan border with off-white scrolls and a row of beading below. A wreath of leaves in greens and mustard, some with overglaze enamel, encircle plate on a cream background to central scroll. A white center with large multicolor floral on the large pieces.

OOELLO MM-34. Gold edge, cream band, then a white band enclosing tulip-like flowers in red with gold outlines. Below are two more gold lines, then a wide cream band to gold center circle outlining the white center. This bread/butter plate from the M. Pettingill collection.

ORADELL 588 MM-38. Gold edge. Brick red scallops above yellow, lined with white background and enclosed by mustard scrolls, outlined in brown. Inner cream band features small multicolor floral bouquets, enclosed in scrolls, alternating with smaller sprays. Border identical to Lares.

PARNELL 302 MM-39. Gold edge scalloped blank with a tan Greek key border. This is a typical Indian Tree pattern with the large central motif. Sample is a berry/sauce dish from the Florence McClain collection.

PEONY 5053 MM-41 Gold edge. Large sprays of peony-type flowers in bright colors with multicolored buds. Leaves are green, aqua and pale blue, and the prominent branches are brown. Pattern dips toward the middle of the plate. Background is all white. China-peony 3060 is the same pattern but in paler colors.

PHOEBE 659, 103008 MM-38. Gold edge. Border design clear-day blue, white and lemon-yellow. Insets of pastel flowers in pink, blue, yellow, with green leaves. Cream background to center scroll in lemon-yellow. White center. See Mystery 109 for similar pattern.

PHYLLIS 318 MM-39. A Dresden-type pattern with gold edge and inner pen line on an all white background. Floral border with flower sprays in two sizes and also a large group in plate center.

PLAZA MM-36. Gold edge, narrow border of dots and beads against a leaf green background and edged with a narrow band of tiny tan dots. Inserts of mustard scrolls and small floral groups in pastel colors. Cream background to bright aqua inner line. White center.

QUEENANNE 4018 MM-38. Gold edge. Wide cream plate rim to gold inner line. Small groups of four different kinds of bright, Dresden-type florals on the cream and a large central bouquet on a white background.

RALEIGH MM-31. Gold edge. In border, reserves of two pink flowers, blue in middle, with white background. Still in border, mustard scroll next to forest green bars, enclosed by mustard bands against white background. Black accent lines and squares. Below on a wide cream band, there is green scrollwork enclosing a light mustard area. Vase bouquets of multicolor blue and pink with touches of mustard are included on cream band down to another elaborate inner narrow band in green, white and mustard. White center. Sample furnished by Mrs. Daniel Quinn.

RENOVIA MM-31. Gold edge. Border of mustard ovals, accented with dark brown, enclose a half flower with brick red center. Two different very bright florals alternate on cream background, the larger floral incorporating a mustard scroll. White center. The arrangement of florals on place setting pieces may vary.

REVENNA 7257, 109493 MM-34. A gold, cream and white pattern. Gold edge and border of circles and leaves with flowers and scrolls on cream background to gold line. White center. This pattern is nearly like Revenna 7270, but the cream background is wider on 7270.

RITZEDO MM-31. Blue border with white circles, black dots and yellow leaves. Inner narrow band of same circle and dots joined by yellow scrolls enclosing pink, yellow and blue floral. All pattern on a cream background. Sample from Mrs. R.L. Raymer's collection.

ROBERTA 593 MM-38. Gold edge. Fern green and yellow scroll border. Multicolored florals, and below these yellow scrolls and flowers form a wreath encircling the plate. Cream background to center scrolls in yellow. White center.

ROCHELLE 675 MM-38. Directly beneath the gold edge is a band of red enclosing white flowers and edged at the bottom with tan scrolls. A wide white area holds multicolored bouquets connected by another chain of tan scrolls extending into a cream background that ends with a tan line encircling the white center of the demitasse saucers.

RODENA MM-38. Gold edge, tan and yellow scrolls enclose the bright green border. Typical bouquets, with yellow scrolls beneath, on cream background to the central scroll line. White center. A bread/butter plate.

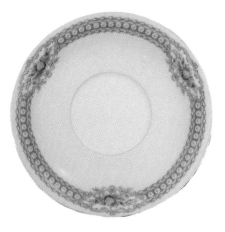

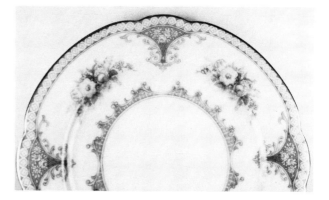

RODISTA 590 MM-38. Gold edge. Cream background to a tan line. Intricate border of bellflowers above and below on ivory and gray band of daisies on a light tan background. Reserves hold dainty florals in multicolors. Saucer pictured.

ROMILLY MM-30. Scalloped blank with gold edge. Narrow band of pale yellow on apple green ground edged in deep yellow. Wide cream band with floral sprays of pink, white, blue, yellow, orange and lavender, with white overglazed touches. Alternating mustard scrolls enclose yellow and tiny white flowers on a green ground. Inner circle is mustard, green and yellow.

ROSEGLOW 86196 MM-31. Gold edge scalloped blank. Tan scrolls enclose a green border with white flowers. Large multicolored flower bouquets on a wide cream background surround the cup. A duplicate bouquet inside the cup is on an all white background.

ROYCE 660 MM-38. Gold edge, clear blue, ivory and pale yellow floral border with groups of flowers interrupting border. Cream background to inner yellow scroll. White center. Not the same pattern as Royce 5809, a later pattern not included in this volume.

143

SABINA MM-31. Outer edge of gold beading, then gold geometric design against white, then a bright green area enclosed by raised gold scrolls and a shield-shaped raised gold design alternating with brilliant floral bouquets on an ivory background to center gold line surrounding white center. A bread/butter plate from Penny Berman's collection.

RUBIGOLD 89501 MM-29. Scalloped blank, gold edge with a feathery gold on white and a wide gold band and gold pen line. Medallion in smaller scallops are ruby red. Cream background to gold pen line. White center. Not the same as Rubigold 4792, a later pattern not pictured in this volume.

SALVADOR 303, 104529 MM-39. Scalloped blank, gold edge. Tan border of scallops and circles. Cream background to inner tan scroll. Atop the cream, delicate pastel florals encircle plate. The crosshatched areas are forget-me-not blue.

SELIKA MM-34. Wide gold geometric design against a cream background. All gold, cream and white.

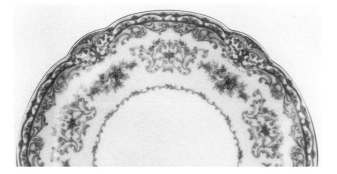

SHELBY 3623 MM-38. Gold edge. Scalloped blank. Green and yellow rim with mustard scrolls. Pattern is multicolored floral sprays alternating with elaborate scrolls and tiny green blossoms circling plate on the cream background to green and mustard inner scroll band. The alternating scroll design is the same decal as is on Mystery 72.

SOMERSET MM-31. Gold scalloped edge. Geometric border of white bells on green background with black darts and below, a yellow background of scallops outlined in black. Recessed are blue scrolls alternating in border with mutlicolor florals with smaller florals in between. Inner band of green vertical bars enclosed by narrow yellow bands, interrupted by blue and yellow leaf scroll. All design on cream background to white center. Not the same pattern as more recent Somerset 5317.

SONORA 3940, 117814 MM-38. Gold edge, maize and orange-yellow band enclosing aquamarine bars. An urn in gray-blue and maize flanked by maize horns of plenty and gray-blue beads and drape. Flowers in urn are rose, orange and pale aqua, with green leaves. A luncheon plate is pictured.

STANFORD 5220 MM-38. Gold edge. Large green leaves with yellow and white spider chrysanthemums on white background encircle plate.

STANWYCK 3913 MM-38. Cornflower blue and pale yellow scrollwork and flowers immediately under the gold edge. Then on a cream background are large multicolored bouquets alternating with smaller florals surrounded by yellow scrolls. Inner line of scrolls bound the white center. This rimmed soup from Adele Peterson's collection.

THERESE 5158 MM-38. Gold edge, wreath of columbine in lavender with green and yellow leaves encircle saucer. All white background.

TIFFANY 95640 MM-36. Gold edge, sea green border with orange-yellow scrolls. Orchid and rose chrysanthemums predominate in a pastel bouquet above yellow scrolls. Cream background to green line demarcating white center.

TOLOA 3841 MM-38. Gold edged scalloped blank. Tan border with ivory and yellow leaf motif interspersed with pale aqua crosses. Below this border, a wreath of leaves and berries with touches of enamel circle the plate on a cream background to the tan inner scrollwork marking off the white center.

TOPAZE 653 MM-38. Gold edged. Yellow and white border outlined with mustard scrolls and flowers with brick red accent dips. Multicolored floral bouquets on a cream background to yellow inner scroll band. White center. Pictured is a square salad plate.

TRIANON 676, 103034 MM-38. Gold edge. Narrow rim of pale yellow enclosing white scrolls and flowers against a Delft blue background. Sprays of blossoms in multicolors with a chain of bright yellow scrolls connecting them is partly on a white background and part on cream background, the cream ending at a hooked-scroll design at white center. A bread/butter plate.

TRINITY MM-38. Gold edge, yellow line, then a side band of wave-shaped motifs in mustard is banded top and bottom with mustard lines, the lower accented with dark tiny scallops. Muticolored florals in an urn and on a cream background to mustard scroll surrounding white center. Pictured is a berry bowl.

VALDINA 3854, 112927, MM-38. Tan leaf border with gray inserts on a scalloped gold-edged blank. A complicated pattern of swags and cameos on a cream background encircles the plate to the line encircling the white center. Pictured is a saucer, the plates may have a scroll border rather than the simple line.

VALIERE 95632 MM-38. Gold edge and inner line where the cream background joins the white center. A black band overlaid with gold design and then a row of gold dots and below that, gold leaves with medallions in gold form the pattern. The pattern 4981 is somewhat more recent and shapes of pieces may differ from the original, but the pattern is identical.

VANITY 3804 MM-38. Gold edge with pale yellow half-circles bordering the gold. A delicate wreath of pale gray-green leaves above a basket and scroll and floral design in multicolors. The basket design is the same as in Nanette. Pictured is a gravy boat.

VENUS MM-31. Gold edge, scalloped blank. Leaf-green fern design surrounds saucer, enclosed by light gray-tan scrolls and band. Flowers are bittersweet and lavender with green leaves. All on cream background to center gold line.

WATTEAU 3735 MM-38. A gold edge tan geometric design forms the outer border and below that on a wide cream band intertwined leaf ropes encircle plate to the white center which is edged in another tan scroll design. Sample from the collection of Lois Johnson.

WILSHIRE 5224 MM-38. Gold edge. Leaves and flowers in gray-yellow and pale olive green encircle plate on white background.

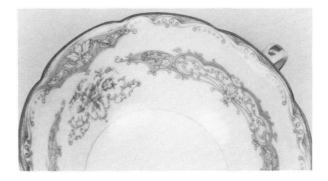

WIMPOLE 3604 MM-38. Gold edge on scalloped blank. A deep border of mustard and white scrolls with blue background and other deeper scrolls holding small floral sprays. Cream background to inner tan line. White center.

WINONA 511 MM-38. Gold edge, white background. Pale lilac, leaves light and dark green. Saucer pictured is from Roberta Bailey's collection.

WROCKLAGE 4706 MM-38, MM-49. Gold edge. Gray and light tan border. Leaves under border are gray. Delicate floral, mostly orchid, rose, white and lavender with gray-tan leaves on cream background to tan line. Often found with no pattern name on pieces.

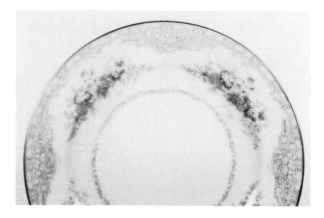

5020 MM-38, MM-41. Gold edge. Yellow, soft dark green and gray-white floral border with brown outlines encircles plate on a cream background to gold inner line. The identifying features are the yellow stamens and small yellow flowers. White center.

98846 MM-39. Gold edge. Tan, maize and ivory floral scroll border with tiny touches of very pale green. Large spray of rose, blue, yellow and red-orange flowers on the cream background to center scrollwork of green and yellow. White center.

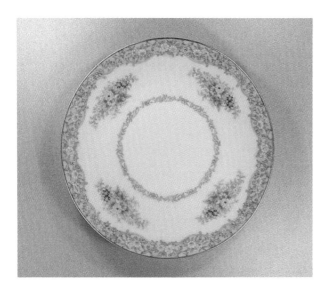

101270 MM-39. Aqua, lemon and orange-yellow border of flowers and scrolls. Flower grouping in multicolors on cream background to fancy inner scroll of aqua and yellow. White center.

MYSTERY 2 MM-39. Gold edge, narrow tan line with brown dots. Lemon-yellow, with touches of tan, scrollwork enclosing spring green areas. Wide cream band with multicolored small and large floral groupings in an alternating fashion. Inner yellow-tan scroll, touched with green line. White center.

MYSTERY 11 MM-39. Gold edge. Green bars and yellow scrolls with flower and leaf sprays interwoven. Multicolor floral sprays on cream background to yellow and green central scroll. White center. Photograph is of a saucer, which does not have the central scroll. This pattern is very similar to Gramatan.

MYSTERY 14 MM-41, MM-45. Design inside cup. Gold edge, leafy scroll band in gray and white against a shaded green background. Wide cream band to a light brown pen line. White center. Central floral is white, outlined in gray with small yellow flowers, gray leaves. Sample furnished by Retha J. Joella.

MYSTERY 15 MM-41. Gold edge. Large roses in dark and light pink with gold leaves on a wide cream band to gold inner line. Center is white.

MYSTERY 18 MM-39. Gold edge, sea green border with yellow scrolls. Pastel bouquets on a cream background to a green line. White center. Saucer is pictured. Other pieces might have a scroll instead of the inner green line.

MYSTERY 20 MM-39. Gold edge. First border has bittersweet and gray-tan scrolls. Second border is light green and gray-tan scrolls. Cream background to tan line. White center. Border is same as in Bellodgia, but colors are different. Pictured is a gravy boat.

MYSTERY 25 MM-39. Gold edge. Maize and light orange-yellow border. Pastel floral bouquets of tiny flowers on cream background to tan line. Saucer pictured. Same border as Mystery 26.

MYSTERY 26 MM-39. Gold edge. Maize and light orange-yellow border. Delicate pastel flower groups connected by elaborate scrolls in border colors. Cream background to brown inner line. White center. Pictured is a saucer from the collection of Lonnie Nicholson.

MYSTERY 30 MM-39. Gold edge, white background with flowers and scrolls shaded light brown, touched with tan. The cream band that follows has multicolor floral bouquets positioned at intervals. A scroll brown-tan line is next. White center. Sample furnished by Jerry Richards.

MYSTERY 33 MM-39. Gold edge, yellow-tan border scroll. Flower groupings in bright multicolors on cream background to inner design of yellow circles. White center.

MYSTERY 46 MM-39. Gold edge, lemon yellow and orange-yellow border interspersed with rose, red-orange and yellow flowers. Wider design beneath is clear day blue with white flowers and scrolls, edged with yellow scrolls. The floral bouquets are mainly thistle, lavender, bittersweet and yellow with bright green leaves. Cream background to tan scroll line. White center.

MYSTERY 50 MM-39. Gold edge. Pale orange-yellow band and light olive design with a touch of black. Yellow, rose, blue and apricot floral with green leaves on cream background to tan line. White center. This border is exactly like Milford, but the florals are different.

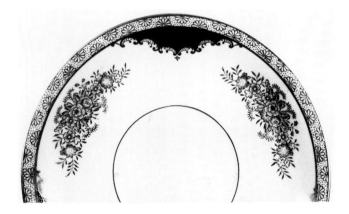

MYSTERY 54 MM-41. Entire pattern gold, black, cream and white. Narrow rim of fan and dot in gold. Gold scrollwork embossed over black alternates with gold flower and leaf sprays.

MYSTERY 57 MM-39. Gold edge has a 1" border of tan and yellow scrollwork and scattered small multicolor flowers on a white background banded at bottom with more scrollwork, and then there is a cream background to tan center line. Sample is from the collection of Fran Driscoll.

MYSTERY 59 MM-37. Leaf green edge. Wide white band with sprays of pastel daisies and bright blue smaller flowers and jade green leaves. A green pen line surrounds a 1" deep ivory band below and the center is white.

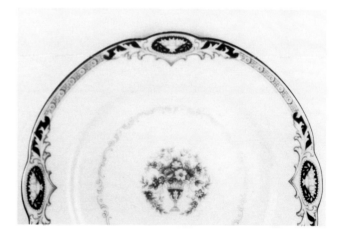

MYSTERY 61 MM-39. Gold edge. Pale orange-yellow border touched with spring green circles and scrolls. Cream background overlaid with baskets of pastel flowers with green and tan scrolls surrounding it. Center white. The basket design is the same as Nanette.

MYSTERY 71 MM-38. Gold edge, scalloped blank. Border is oxblood red behind a compote of fruit in ivory, trimmed with beading and ox-blood red behind brown and ivory scrolls. White circles on a tan background connect the larger motifs. Cream background to tan scroll and white center. Center vase is lavender and yellow filled with a multicolored bouquet.

MYSTERY 72 MM-39. Gold edge, tan and yellow scroll border with white flowers. Beneath this, bright florals alternate with elaborate scroll designs in yellow and pale green (see Shelby for same scroll design). Cream background to tan pen line. White center.

MYSTERY 89 MM-39. Gold edge. Mustard and white roses and scrolls with small tan insets against a green background. Wide cream band holds mustard yellow scrolls and multicolored floral sprays that alternate with smaller floral groupings. Center white.

MYSTERY 94 MM-39. Gold edge. White ropelike border on a bright blue band edged in yellow scrolls and three small yellow flowers at intervals. See Ivanhoe for the same border. Inner design, on cream background, has flowers in bright yellow vases. Inner circle is of gray-blue scallops. White center.

MYSTERY 87 MM-38. Scalloped blank with a gold edge. Narrow border of white scrollwork. Below this a mustard and light brown scroll band, then a wider band of brown scrolls, swags and medallions with pink, blue, orange and yellow flowers and green leaves. Design is on the usual cream background to inner mustard line. White center.

MYSTERY 92 MM-33. Gold edge. Large hand-painted floral in blue and lavender with green leaves.

MYSTERY 105 MM-39. Gold edge. Bright green and deep yellow geometric border. Bright yellow swags with insets of lavender and gray-blue. Below this, multicolored flowers and fruit in a basket, all on cream background to green line. White center. From a coupe underplate.

MYSTERY 109 MM-39. Gold edge. Narrow rim and all scrolls in beige and light mustard. Wide cream border with bright floral groups alternating with a pattern of scrolls against a sky-blue ground. Tan inner line. Medallion and scroll part of the design is identical to that of Phoebe. From a cup.

MYSTERY 110 MM-39. Gold edge, tan scroll border accented with rust red. Alternating florals, one large and one small, in typical pastels. Cream background to tan scroll. White center.

MYSTERY 112 MM-38. Gold edge. Scalloped blank. Border of blue-green, lozenge-shaped bars surrounded by narrow tan bands and half-circle. Scroll designs in smaller scallops are in the same colors. A wreath of large flowers in blue, green, yellow and rust encircles plate. All on a white background. Very similar to Norwich and Cyril.

MYSTERY 142 MM-39. Gold edge, orange area to scallops. Wide cream band with small flowers. Next, an inner border of tan, white and touch of orange scrolls outlined in brown. Motif of multicolor flower bouquets of pink, white, orange, yellow and blue with green leaves. Next, tan scroll line and white center. Sample furnished by Sylvia Rasmussen.

MYSTERY 143 MM-39. Gold edge, blue band with leaf and shell motif. Under the shells are typical Noritake bouquets in multicolors on a cream background to center circle of blue. A saucer from Mrs. Sam Feiwell's collection.

MYSTERY 144 MM-34. Gold design on a cream band and white center. A saucer is pictured.

MYSTERY 145 MM-39. Gold edge and below this, orange, green and tan connected by tan inserts in first border. Then the wide cream border overlaid with pastel florals and scrolls which completely encircle this soup bowl. Fancy green and yellow inner circle bounds the white center.

MYSTERY 146 MM-39. Gold edge. Red and tan scalloped line, then a row of green leaves and tiny fleur de lis. Below, on the cream background and nearly encircling the dish, are multicolored florals and scrolls. The white center is bordered by a scrollwork design in tan.

MYSTERY 147 MM-39. Gold edge. Light green background with shell and scroll design in tan. Floral sprays alternate with an elaborate large scroll in tan and yellow to encircle saucer on a cream background to tan line. White center. Saucer submitted by Dee LaMonica.

MYSTERY 148 MM-39. Gold edge. Yellow and mustard scrolls alternate with flower insets to compose border. Muticolor flower and scroll motifs are superimposed on the cream background to a mustard scroll circle banding the white center.

MYSTERY 149 MM-39. Gold edge. Yellow and brown scroll border. Flower bouquets, in a scroll urn and on the cream background, are just the same as Milford 89486. Sample furnished by Margarita Luna.

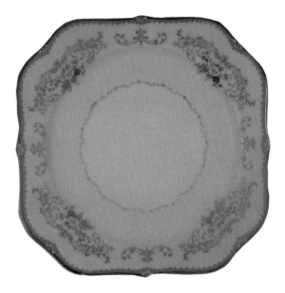

MYSTERY 150 MM-39. Gold, orange and green lines with tan scroll for border. Delicate florals with much scrolling on the cream background completes the pattern to the yellow and green center circle surrounding white center. A square salad furnished by Mr. and Mrs. W. Bradley.

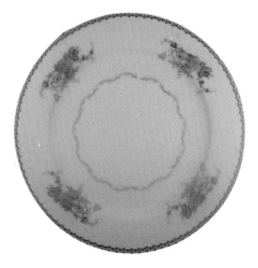

MYSTERY 152 MM-40. Gold edge. White and tan flowers against a green area enclosed by tan scroll with medallion inserts compose the border. Multicolored flowers on cream background to tan scroll line and white center.

MYSTERY 153 MM-39. Gold edge. Geometric border of muticolor bouquets on a cream background to inner scroll in yellow and green surrounding white center.

MYSTERY 154 MM-39. Gold edge. Yellow and tan scroll border. On a cream background, bouquets of flowers, the larger of the two motifs, almost encircled with yellow scrolls. Pictured is a sugar bowl, unfortunately its lid is missing. Sample is from Myra Rosenthal's collection.

MYSTERY 155 MM-39. Gold edge. Narrow black band with white dots and yellow area followed by a narrow green band, compose the border. Multicolor floral against a cream background to an aqua line demarcating the white center.

MYSTERY 156 MM-39. Gold edge, geometric design in a green border. Muticolor florais and fruit in a blue vase on a cream border to blue-green line. A saucer pictured.

MYSTERY 157 MM-39. Gold edge. Orange area with delicate white flowers enclosed by green scroll. Large well-separated florals with scrolling on a cream background to center ring of fancy scrolls in orange and green. Pictured is a bread/butter plate.

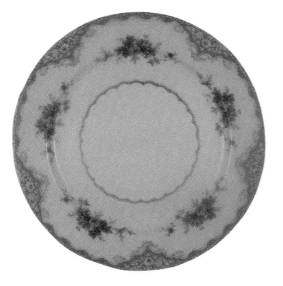

MYSTERY 159 MM-39. Gold edge. Rope border of tan and white, against green area. Pattern of two different multicolored florals and yellow scrolls against the cream background with a central scroll of green and yellow circling the white center. (Reported to be identified as Acalon.) A bread/butter plate from collection of Mrs. Pierce Sherman.

MYSTERY 158 MM-39. Gold edge. Gray-beige border with white flowers. Multicolored florals on a cream background to scalloped center scroll. A dinner plate pictured.

MYSTERY 161 MM-38. Gold edge. Large red and gold leaves to gold line. All on white background. Sample of a saucer from the collection of Mrs. Robert Gorechi.

MYSTERY 160 MM-39. Gold edge. Green area with yellow scallops and scrolls with green dots make up border. Scalloped center scroll with floral groups in multicolors on cream background to white center.

MYSTERY 162 MM-39. Gold edge. Dark green-gray area with light green-gray scallops and scrollwork enclosing tan and white flowers. Multicolor flower bouquets on cream background to mustard scroll line. Center is white. Jean Walsh's collection. A square salad plate.

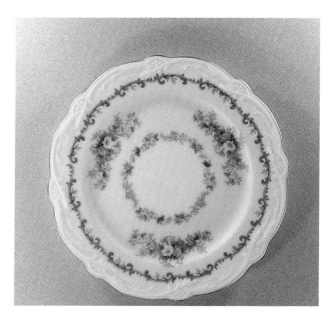

MYSTERY 163 MM-39. Gold edge scalloped blank. White embossed scroll band to tan scrollwork. Then on a cream background, large floral groups on an elaborate wine scroll circling the white center. A bread/butter plate.

MYSTERY 164 MM-41. Gold trim. Large wildflower floral motif in orange, lavender, yellow and blue on a white background.

MYSTERY 165 MM-41. Gold outer band border with a cream background to a second inner gold band. Very soft pink, yellow, gray and dark green in flower bouquet motif. Sample bread/butter plate furnished by Isabel Catogge.

MYSTERY 166 MM-41. Gold trim. Bright pink rose and green leaves make a border on the white background of this bread and butter plate. Sample furnished by Betty Hauenstein.

MYSTERY 180 MM-37. Gold edge. Cream band to sprays of flower bouquets and swag florals connecting bouquets on a white background. Mustard inner line demarcating white center. A bread and butter plate.

MYSTERY 187 MM-31. Yellow-tan border with dark blue scallops below. A handsome pattern with birds in pink, blue, and gray flank a blue urn filled with fruits and flowers. Another urn without birds alternates. Two pen lines of dark blue separate the pattern from the white center. A saucer courtesy of J.J. Chandler.

MYSTERY 188 MM-41. A white plate banded in gold with a gold pen line below. Pink daisies with burgundy stamens and two shades of green foliage form a circular pattern in the center of this coupe shaped bread and butter plate.

MYSTERY 189 MM-41. Turkey platter has a gold edge and mock handles with gold striping. A wide cream band continuing all around the pieces is decorated with many different kinds and colors of garden flowers. Inner scroll is a small border of yellow figures outlined with black dots. White center. Sample from the Susan Hirshman collection.

MYSTERY 190 MM-39. Gold edge. Yellow and mustard scroll border with pale green and white half flowers. On the cream background are floral sprays, topped with yellow scrollwork and pale green leaves. Border surrounding white center is yellow and tan scallops and dots. A bread and butter plate.

MYSTERY 191 MM-37. Gold edge. Sections of cross-hatching against aqua background with white flowers, enclosed by tan scrolls, are interrupted by multicolored florals that compose the border. Then a wide cream band to a tan pen line after which is a white center. Sample from collection of June J. Time.

MYSTERY 192 MM-41. Gold edge. Thistles in pink, yellow, gray and brown form a border around this creamer. All white background.

MYSTERY 193 MM-39. Gold edge. Tan geometric border with red darts and insets of roses. Below, on a cream background, are larger matching multicolored florals to tan scrolling surrounding all white center area.

MYSTERY 194 MM-39. Gold edge. Light green background with tan and white scrollwork and crosshatching. Next, elaborate section of tiny florals and leaves in yellow and tan with darker scrolls at bottom, and finally, all on cream background, multicolor bouquets to the tan pen line demarcating white center. Sample furnished by Dorothy W. Barnett.

MYSTERY 195 MM-38. Scalloped gold edge with brick red darts, small line of beading and yellow multicolored bouquets on a cream background to the tan line encircling white center. Sample furnished by Susie Wasserman.

MYSTERY 196 MM-38. Gold edge. White background. Border of large peonies in bright pink and white, smaller flowers in pink and yellow, berries and buds in orange and prominent green and blue leaves. The size of the piece determines the size of the pattern.

MYSTERY 197 MM-39. Gold edge. Green border underlined with much yellow scrollwork touched with green. Large florals in delicate colors on the cream background to yellow scalloped scrolls surrounding the white center. Sample furnished by Patricia Klauck.

MYSTERY 198 MM-39. Gold edge. Mustard and yellow scroll border underlined with tiny light green leaves. Multicolor floral with mustard scroll on the cream background to white center, outlined with yellow scrolls. Fragment of a berry bowl submitted by Elvera M. Bierlein.

MYSTERY 211 MM-39. Gold edge, white embossed area to a tan scalloped band containing white flowers. Superimposed on a wide cream band are large and small flower groupings of multicolor which surround the piece, ending with a tan scroll line. White center.

MYSTERY 213 MM-39. Gold edge. Scroll border of mustard green and pink, outlined in black. Superimposed on a wide cream background are floral bouquets of pink flowers, touched with yellow and green leaves to an inner tan pen line. White center. Sample furnished by Ruth Ilgen.

MYSTERY 214 MM-39. Gold edge, pale tan-orange border with white circles and scrolls within. Next is a wide cream border, overlaid with a design of multicolor florals and scrollwork, touched with green. White center.

MYSTERY 215 MM-39. Gold edge, thin yellow line, lime green background, white daisies within and surrounded by yellow-tan scrolls. On a wide cream band are alternating large and small multicolor floral groups to a tan-yellow scroll line. White center.

MYSTERY 217 MM-39. Gold edge, narrow cream border with repeating white flower against tan-orange area. A design line separates this border from a broad cream band. Multiflorals of pink, rust, blue, white and orange, with yellow-tan scroll, appear also on the cream band, then a tan-orange pen line demarcating the white center.

MYSTERY 234 MM-39. Gold edge. Light blue border enclosing white flowers alternating with yellow and white scroll areas and below that are floral bouquets with scrollwork beneath. Cream background to white center bordered with more scrolls. A bread and butter plate from Cath Posehn's collection.

MYSTERY 235 MM-39. Gold edge. Green and pale yellow scroll border and below that, large and small floral sprays in pink and yellow with green leaves on a cream background to yellow and brown central scrolls, outlining the white center. Sample from James Cleveland's collection.

MM-42

MM-44

MM-45

MM-46

MM-47

MM-48

MM-42. 1940. Handpainted; appears in brown, green, and yellow.

MM-43. Similar to MM-42, but omits word "handpainted." (Not shown).

MM-44. 1940. Similar to MM-37, but has "M-in-wreath" mark, rather than "N-in-wreath."

MM-45. 1947 to 1949; this stamp was registered in the United States in 1950. Note the "spoke-in-scroll" and the word "Noritake" in script. Appears in green, tan, and mustard.

MM-46. Registry in Japan in 1946. Pink roses, green leaves, and black letters. One of several stamps used for china made in occupied Japan.

MM-47. 1949. Made during the occupation period; is the same stamp as MM-45 and frequently referred to as the "spoke-in-scroll."

MM-48. 1947 to 1950. This stamp is the same as the prewar MM-27, but with "Occupied Japan." The same pattern, 175, is in current production, with a U.S. patent registry date of 1949. All in gold.

MM-49

MM-50

MM-51

MM-52

MM-53

MM-54

MM-49. Circa 1949. This is the same stamp as MM-38 and MM-41, and appears in the same colors.

MM-50. Circa 1949. This stamp was adapted from the earlier stamp MM-9. However, this backmark with the additional slogan "Nippon Toki Kaisha" (which translates: "Japan's Finest China") confirms that this use of the word "Nippon" does not indicate "old" Nippon — a common misconception.

MM-51. Circa 1949 to 1950. This the same stamp as MM-45 and MM-47.

MM-52. Pre-1952. Another Rose China stamp in the same colors as MM-46. Pattern discarded and name and number reissued later.

MM-53. Pre-1952. Name and number reissued.

MM-54. Originally issued in Japan in 1914 and registered in India in 1926. Reissued in Japan in 1950. Royal Crockery appears in black, with dull gray-green leaf spray.

MM-55

MM-56

MM-57

MM-58

MM-59

MM-60

MM-55. Pre-1953. Brown R.C. letters with pale brown striping in the background. Green leaf sprays. The last of the Royal Crockery marks. Some of these latter patterns were discarded, while others were reissued under United States registry in the 1960's.

MM-56. Circa 1952. Scroll is in beige and brown on an ivory background, with black lettering.

MM-57. Circa 1950. Same stamp as MM-38 etc., and in the same color range. The last appearance of the Morimura "M-in-wreath," here with the insertion of the circled R, indicating registration in the United States.

MM-58. Circa 1953. "N-in-wreath" with bow now replaces "M-in-wreath," as in MM-57, but with "Made in Japan" added.

MM-59. Circa 1953 to 1964. Same stamp, same colors, but with "Japan" only.

MM-60. 1953 to present. With circled R denoting registry in the United States, as well as Japan.

PATTERNS 1940 TO 1955

In our last section, we find the introduction of the silver and platinum trimmed patterns.

AMHERST 501 MM-45. Large carnations in pink and orchid with touches of rose and yellow appear to drop from the gold edge down into the white plate. Fern green foliage and some gray. This is the same decal as Mystery 1 but with cream band and tan line.

AUDREY 3078 MM-45. Gold edge. White and black Greek key geometric border with rickrack effect below, on cream background to the gold line surrounding white center.

CAMELOT 3031, 6000, 117817 MM-45. Gold edge. Blue-green and lemon yellow scrolls in border. Large floral bouquets in rose, olive green, bittersweet and blue on cream background to inner tan scrolls. White center. Shapes of some pieces differ from #6000, and also placement of the design on the cup, but patterns are the same.

CHEVONIA 6003 MM-44. Gold edge. Mustard scrollwork encloses multicolored floral insets in a vase and connected by a wide blue band with white scrollwork and edged at the bottom with mustard scrolls and tracery. Inner scroll circle of the same color. This pattern also comes with no name on it, mark MM-45 (made in Occupied Japan).

CORDOVA 5215 MM-57, MM-41, MM-38. Gold edge, brown line, all white. Wreath of large green and brown leaves and brown-purple berries encircle plate with group in center. Pieces with back stamps 41 and 38 have no brown line but are otherwise the same.

DRESDLINA MM-42. Dresden-type bouquets on an all-white background with gold scroll at gold edge. Flowers are rose, bittersweet, violet, bright blue and yellow, with blue-green and yellow leaves. A bread and butter plate pictured.

DRESDOLL 4716 MM-42. Gold edge and fancy gold scroll border. Bright Dresden-type scattered floral includes a yellow and lavender iris and a bittersweet tulip in center.

DRESITA 4733 MM-49. Gold edge, gold scroll border. Alternating multicolor floral groups, one large and one small. Dresden type pattern.

DULCY 5153 MM-57. Gold edge. Scattered florals of orange flowers and tan leaves and gold leaves. All white background.

GARNET 5656 Made for Australian market, probably after 1950. Gold geometric design at edge incorporating touches of white. Wide red band with superimposed leaf design. An ivory band to the gold pen line demarcating the white center. From Margot Stengel's collection.

GEORGETTE 305 MM-44. Gold rim, red band and brown leaf spray. Large flower spray on cream background to tan line. This pattern identical to Mariposa 319.

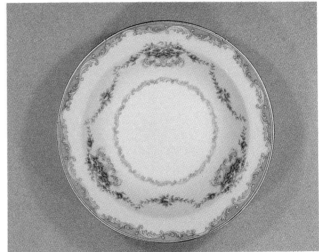

GREENBRIAR 4730 MM-57. Gold edge. Spring green and pale yellow scrolls in border. Multicolored florals in an urn. Swags of pink roses and green leaves connect the urn motif to encircle plate. Cream background to inner yellow and green scroll line which demarcates white center. This pattern was listed as Mystery 49, but has since been identified.

LAVETA 513 MM-45. Gold edge and inner line. Large flowers in bright yellow with stamens in deep yellow and buds in yellow-green, touched with light brown. Stems green.

MARGARITA 5049 MM-57. Gold edge, wide light gray band to darker gray pen line. White center. Center motif is large flower in colors of pink, gray, with touches of yellow-orange in centers and leaves in shades of green.

MARGOT 5605 MM-57. Silver edge. White band, then blue-gray pen line make up the all white piece with a center rose and bud motif. Rose petals are brown-gray with red and gray center, leaves are gray-green. Pictured is a coupe shape salad plate.

MARIPOSA 319 MM-44. Please see Georgette 305 for description. Both patterns look identical but names and numbers are on both. This could be a manufacturing mistake.

MAYWOOD 5154 MM-57. Gold edge. Border design of blue ribbon streamers alternating with pink and yellow rose sprays all on the diagonal. This pattern is listed as Amywood in the Noritake Supplement.

NANCY (Rose China) 3402 MM-53. Platinum edge. Pale pink roses and gray-green leaves and brown stems. Different from Nancy 5163, not pictured.

RAMONA 6504, 118708 MM-44. Gold edge. Tan and maize scroll border also forms reserves holding bright multicolored floral sprays. Other larger floral sprays alternate on the cream background to tan pen line. White center has large floral spray in middle. This pattern is reminiscent of the Dresden-type patterns. Not same as Ramona 5203, not pictured.

RANSDELL 3004 MM-45. Gold edge. Tan and white leaves against green background enclosed by tan scrolls compose the border. Typical Noritake flower sprays against a cream background to tan scroll marking off white center.

REDLACE 3024 MM-45, MM-47. Gold edge. Mustard and brick-red banded pattern, with a row of dots beneath, alternate with typical Noritake floral on the cream background to tan scrolls surrounding white center. This bread and butter plate does not have name or pattern number on it. Sample furnished by Ann Doogan. A re-issue of an older pattern.

NOT PICTURED:

REMEMBRANCE 5146 MM-57. Gold edge. Two rows of small blue sprays, alternating with gold fleur-de-lis, on all white background. Inner pen line of gold.

ROSALIE 3052 MM-45. Gold edge. All white background, two rows of scattered pink roses with green leaves, alternate with gold leaves. Gold pen line in center.

ROSEBUD 6002 MM-44. Red areas in mustard border just below gold edge. Large flower bouquets in a vase form a part of the border on a cream background to a tan and mustard scroll work. White center. There is a much later pattern named "Melrose" that was given the same number 6002, which is not within the scope of this book.

ROSELACE 5041 MM-57. Gold edge. All white background. Pink and white roses with leaves in colors of green, blue and green-yellow, with brown branches, surround the entire piece. Next is an inner gold line.

ROSELANE 5147 MM-57. Gold edge. Large flowers in violet, pink and gray encircle the plate. All white background with a gold inner line.

ROSEMONT 5048 MM-58. Gold edge. Large gray band, then a gray-brown wreath of leaves encircling all white background with a rose motif in colors of pink, white and yellow with brown-gray leaves in center.

SANDRA 3062 MM-45. Gold edge. White background. Central motif starting near edge to length of 3½" with yellow, rust and blue flowers and green leaves. Also, a small group of similar flowers on upper left of motif.

SANFORD 5860 MM-59. Silver edge. White narrow area, then a silver pen line compose border. All white piece. The center motif is a gray pussy willow with black stems.

SHARON 3057 MM-45. Gold edge. White narrow band, then a gold pen line compose border. All white with center motif of pink rose with buds surrounded by green and yellow-green leaves.

SHASTA 5305 MM-59. Silver edge. Pale green band to silver pen line. Flowers and leaves in center are muted lavender, yellow and gray, against a white background.

SHELBURNE 5316 MM-59. Gold edge. Border of small gray scallops and tan and white leaves on gray. A swag of tan roses with green and gray leaves surrounds the cup. An inner gold pen line and an all white background.

SIERRA ROSE 3308 MM-53. Gold edge. Wreath of a delicate rose vine with pink roses and buds encircle the cup. An all white background.

SOMERSET 5317 MM-59. Gold edge. Border of tan leaves and flowers enclosing gray background, touched with darker gray leaves. The remainder of the piece is white with multicolor florals superimposed. A gold pen line around center.

STANWYCK 5818 MM-57. Gold edge. All white plate with border of scrolled leaves of gold and pale blue. An extra pen line around edge and one just below the border.

TOURAINE 3025 MM-45. Gold edge. All white with floral sprays of gray, white, pink and blue flowers.

VIOLETTE 3054 MM-45. Gold edged white china with an encircling wreath of blue and pale lavender violets. A center motif of the same flowers inside a gold pen line.

1802 MM-51. Gold edge. Brick red bars and tan flowers in border. Tan and yellow scrolls and swags encircle plate and incorporate a floral medallion. Cream background to tan inner circle. White center.

5612 MM-51. Gold edge. All white body, with pine branches as a motif. Brown branches, green pine needles and gold patches arranged. Collection of Linda McMenimon.

MYSTERY 1 MM-44. Gold edge. Large carnations in pink and orchid, touched with rose and yellow. Fern green and gray foliage on a cream background to tan pen line and white center. Amherst 501 has the same pattern on an all white background.

MYSTERY 3 MM-50. The MM-50 mark is in maroon. Gold edge. Watermelon pink background with large gray and white roses.

MYSTERY 7 MM-49. Gold edge. Forget-me-not blue border with white daisies within and pale tan scrolls beneath. Cream background to tan center scroll. Multi-color floral bouquets. White center.

MYSTERY 10 MM-42. Gold edge. Border of grape leaves, vines and grapes in white with deep yellow veining on a blue ground. Deep yellow scrolls enclose multicolor floral groups.

MYSTERY 24 MM-47. Gold edge. Indian red border with white leaves. Pastel bouquets on a cream background to tan line. White center.

MYSTERY 27 MM-47. Gold edge. Light blue and greenish yellow border with black medallions. Multicolor floral bouquets on cream background to tan line. This pattern has identical border to Mystery 68 and Romance.

MYSTERY 36 MM-49. Gold edge, sepia background with ivory circles. A brick red band enclosing ivory scrollwork. Motif is a fan draped floral of pink, lavender and brown shades on a cream band. White body.

MYSTERY 37 MM-44. Gold edge. Multicolor floral alternating with medallion in blue and yellow. Cream background to yellow scroll surrounding white center.

MYSTERY 39 MM-44. Gold edge. Fern green border design with white flowers alternating with pastel bouquets. Cream background to tan line. White center.

MYSTERY 44 MM-44. Gold edge. Light brown border area with cream flowers enclosed by yellow scrolls. Cream background to light brown line. White center. Multicolored floral motif of pink, orange and yellow above tan-yellow scrolls. From the collection of Kathy Buss.

MYSTERY 45 MM-44. Gold edge. Bright violet areas with white flowers edged in yellow scrolls alternate with florals in bright colors. Yellow and tan scrolls separate cream background from white center. Another version of this same pattern with mark MM-45 has a different arrangement of flowers in the floral and major design inside the cup.

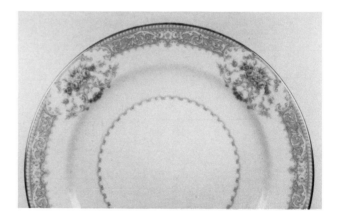

MYSTERY 48 MM-47. Gold edge. Gold scroll design. Bouquets of Dresden-type colorful flowers. All on white background.

MYSTERY 55 MM-45. Gold edge. Gray-tan and light tan circles and scrolls in border. A vase with orchid to maroon roses flanking a yellow flower and smaller flowers in blue, yellow and pink. Cream ground to tan scroll.

MYSTERY 56 MM-44, MM-45, MM-47. Gold edge. Rich tan border enclosing ivory design and edged with green-gray scrolls. Multicolored floral in a gray vase with gray scrolls. Cream ground to tan line. Also comes with blue-gray scrolls beneath the border.

MYSTERY 58 MM-49. Gold edge. The border is mustard and pale apple green. Floral sprays of two kinds in the usual color palette appear on a cream background to a mustard inner ring. Center white. From a cup.

MYSTERY 67 MM-47. Gold edge. Light brown and ivory circles above a pale blue border with ivory scrolls and flowers. Pastel floral inserts in a tan vase surrounded by scrolls. Similar to Chevonia. See Mystery 55 for description of different color variation.

MYSTERY 68 MM-51. Rust colored edge. Narrow cream band, light blue and yellow border design with black medallions. Multicolor floral bouquets on cream background to tan line. This pattern also appears with a gold edge.

MYSTERY 77 MM-44. Gold edge. Cream background to tan line. Bright floral groups alternate with yellow scroll groups, which have small floral swags beneath the center scroll medallions. White center.

MYSTERY 85 MM-54. Platinum edge and inner line below. Fern fronds in center in four shades of green. A later pattern.

MYSTERY 88 MM-45. Gold edge. Wide beige border with lighter small flowers. Insets of small multicolored florals on a white background. Cream band to inner beige scrollwork. White center.

MYSTERY 100 MM-47. Gold edge. Blue border with tan to cream bars and flowers Below border, on cream background, are typical florals in multicolors with tan scrolls. Inner ring is tan.

MYSTERY 102 MM-44. Gold edge. Wide scroll band in mustard and yellow-green against a white background broken by small multicolored floral sprays. Wide cream band to tan inner line.

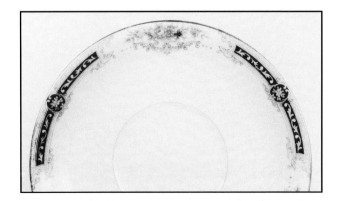

MYSTERY 103 MM-47. Gold edge. Narrow geometric band in tan and beige, and beneath this, scrolls against an oxblood red background alternating with colorful sprays of flowers enclosed in beige scrolls. Tan inner line.

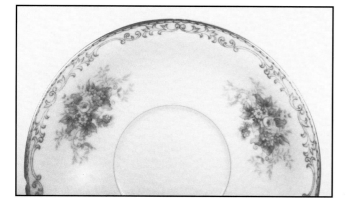

MYSTERY 113 MM-43. Gold edge. Tiny rim of pea-green scallops and mustard scrolls. Large groups of multi-colored flowers with yellow scrollwork and pale gray-blue shadow foliage. Inner tan line. Border is like Aberdale and Mimi.

MYSTERY 114 MM-58, MM-59. Two color variations of the same pattern, both with gold edges, mustard scrolls and rose rim borders. One variation is against a robin's egg blue ground and the other against a pale green background. Florals in both are identical mustard vases, scrolls and swags, with flowers in rose, orange, lavender and purple with green and lavender leaves.

MYSTERY 117 MM-44. Gold edge. Wide cream band ending in a tan line to white center. Bright floral sprays of pink roses and rust zinnia alternate with pale orange, tan and green scrollwork which also includes a leaf design and small pink roses.

MYSTERY 119 MM-56. Brown edge. Turquoise blue border. Typical florals with scrollwork above alternating groups. Cream background to inner circular scroll. Cup is slightly taller and narrower than the old LaSalle shape (our Cup Shape 1). Pattern on outside of cup. Same pattern as Colby 5032, except that Colby has gold edge and pattern inside cup.

MYSTERY 167 MM-42. Gold design on cream and white.

MYSTERY 168 MM-42. All gold leaf border and motif design on cream and white.

MYSTERY 169 MM-42. Gold edge. Aqua band of florals with tan geometric band below. Large floral groups on a cream band to white center.

MYSTERY 170 MM-42. Gold edge. Solid yellow, white inside. This cup may be part of a teaset with assorted solid cups.

MYSTERY 171 MM-47. Gold edge. Blue border outlined with band of pale yellow and incorporating a beaded cameo design. The larger motifs are bouquets of flowers in a tan vase with much scrollwork in tan. The cream background extends to a scalloped scroll in tan and the center is white. From Trudy Huber's collection.

MYSTERY 173 MM-47. Gold edge. Mustard and red border with an almost continuous multicolored floral wreath on cream ground to tan scrollwork and white center. Furnished by Jim Johnson and Christine Hefner.

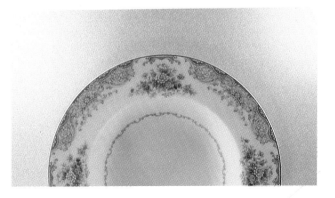

MYSTERY 177. MM-45. Gold edge. Green and white scallops to complex scroll and flower design. Yellow and tan compose the border. At intervals, on border are the floral bouquets, all on cream background. Tan scroll line to white center. Furnished by Pam Wood.

MYSTERY 175 MM-47. Gold edge. Red border with tan scrolls on a cream ground. Superimposed are the typical Noritake florals. Center is white surrounded by tan scrollwork. Mary Roy's and Mrs. Joe Jilderda's collection.

MYSTERY 176 MM-44. Gold edge. Touch of red in border. Tan scrolls containing orange squares with white circles on a wide cream band. There are also the typical Noritake bouquets in multicolors. Tan scrolls surround the white center. From Joy Green.

MYSTERY 178 MM-45. Gold edge. White background with pink and paler pink flowers, gray leaves and yellow berries. One of our customers has told us this is the pattern Clayton 502; however, we have not confirmed this.

MYSTERY 179 MM-46. Gold edge. Tan scallops, red area with tan and mustard leaves compose border. Typical Noritake florals on a cream ground to inner scroll surrounding white center.

MYSTERY 200 MM-45. Gold edge. Border composed of dull aqua geometric design on white ground. Below, a narrow tan band, cream pen line and tan scallops. A repeating design of blue and green scrollwork with a tan vessel holding flowers at the top. The motifs are connected by leaf swags directly beneath fleur-de-lis scrolls on a cream band. White center. Furnished by Pat Kosconski.

MYSTERY 201 MM-47. Gold edge. Burgundy and tan border with white leaves. Alternating are scrolled vase floral bouquets opening into a wide cream band. Tan scroll line surrounds white center. Furnished by Jackie Kelley.

MYSTERY 202 MM-51. One of the few patterns in this age group with a platinum edge. Green pine trees with gray-brown trunks form the pattern, touched with a bit of pale blue sky and gray-brown earth.

MYSTERY 203 MM-45. Gold edge. Red and white geometric border. Gray-tan florals in urns form part of the border. All on a cream background to white center surrounded by mustard scrollwork. Center bouquet in shades of lavender and blue with olive leaves. Sample furnished by Jerry Richards. Border of Acton 4001 is the same.

MYSTERY 204 MM-50. Gold edge. White with bamboo in two shades of green. Sample from Zelma Boyles.

MYSTERY 205 MM-45. Gold edge. White leaves and flowers surrounded by tan scrolls against brick red background compose the border. Insets of floral bouquets are also incorporated, flowing onto a cream band to tan pen line. White center. Sample from Forrest A. Oldenburg.

MYSTERY 206 MM-47. Gold edge. The rich tan scroll and flower border has large florals in urn on a cream background to tan pen line. Sample furnished by Jean Stark.

MYSTERY 207 MM-44. Gold edge. Areas of green background containing white flowers and beneath that, yellow scrolls alternate with typical Noritake bouquets around the piece. Cream background to tan inner line circling the white center. Sample furnished by Hedda Wright and Lois Johnson. The same pattern comes in blue where green is pictured, and also in red.

MYSTERY 208 MM-49. Gold edge. Elaborate scroll border in tan, with touches of dark red, alternate with flower sprays to form the border. Cream background to white center separated by tan scrollwork. Sample furnished by Chris Des Marais.

MYSTERY 209 MM-44. Gold edge. Touches of red in border with yellow scrolling and large floral bouquets. Two different motifs alternating. All on cream background to center yellow scroll. White center. Sample furnished by Thelma Brookens.

MYSTERY 210 MM-44. Gold edge. Pale yellow border incorporating urns of fruit and white flowers against a turquoise background. Alternating floral bouquets on cream background to tan line. All white center. Sample furnished by Bonnie Thompson.

MYSTERY 218 MM-46. Gold edge. Narrow yellow line, light blue and yellow design outlined in black with black medallions, on wide cream band. Multicolored floral groupings in orange, white, yellow and blue are superimposed on the cream band to tan pen line. White center.

MYSTERY 219 MM-51. Gold edge. Wide cream band, inner gold pen line. A wreath of gray tone leaves surround the piece, all on a white ground with a center motif of a pink rose and bud touched with yellow and leaves of gray.

MYSTERY 220 MM-45. Gold edge. A wide cream band with a hue of green. Wreath of green leaves and white flowers surround the piece on a white ground. Central motif, dogwood flowers in white, touched with orange and leaves in different shades of green.

MYSTERY 221 MM-41. Gold edge. Border composed of wide gray band to a darker inner pen line. Swags of pink flowers and gray-green leaves surround the piece on a white center. Sample furnished by Doris Sutton.

MYSTERY 222 MM-43. Gold edge. Thin band of tan-orange with half florals in white. Directly attached are leaves of white and tan. A wide cream band follows, with three or more floral sprays in pink, yellow, orange, with green and yellow-green leaves. A brown pen line to white center. Sample from Jackie Gardiner.

OLD NORITAKE PATTERNS IN NUMERICAL ORDER

In many cases, the older Noritake patterns bear only the number and not the name of the pattern in the backmark. The following list in numerical order will help in identifying each pattern by name, thus enabling you to find the picture in the alphabetical list. In cases where no name is given in the list, you can find the picture in the numbered section.

There are a few numbered patterns for which we had no suitable sample to photograph, but all numbers given here have been verified from customer samples submitted to us.

D167	Garland (also 95633)	615	Cereus	3054	Violette
175	White and Gold (also 16034)	620	Lavegas	3057	Sharon
193	Cardinal (also 98829)	622	Bluedawn (also 100331, 4715)	3062	Sandra
302	Parnell	631	Lolita	3078	Audrey
303	Salvador (also 104529)	651	Allard	3308	Sierra Rose
305	Georgette	652	Hermione	3402	Nancy
318	Phyllis	653	Topaze	3604	Wimpole
319	Mariposa	655	Cynthia	3623	Shelby
370	Melrose	657	Claire (also 103007)	3642	Hyannis
469	Goldream	659	Phoebe (also 103008)	3700	Malibu
470	Goldcrest	660	Royce	3702	Musetta
483	Fiesta	661	Oberon	3705	Ada
501	Amherst	673	Nerrisa (also 103009; on	3708	Decamps
502	Eureka		some pieces, the same pattern	3709	Stratford
503	Arabella		is spelled Nerissa)	3720	Bassano
509	Acacia (also 98212)	674	Naomi (repeated as 4901;	3721	Alexis (also 108369)
511	Winona		shapes differ)	3723	Gellee
513	Laveta	675	Rochelle	3725	Durer
515	Merida	676	Trianon (also 103034)	3727	Ribera
520	Alameda	678	Leslie	3730	Raphael
525	Linden (also 98217)	680	Oympia	3732	Coypel (also 108374)
582	Hampton	682	Nanarosa (repeated as 4902 and	3733	Caliban
583	Claudia		Occupied Japan)	3735	Watteau
584	Joan	683	Nanette	3744	Ciro (also 108378)
585	Jasmine	684	Fabian	3754	Laramie
586	Allure	685	Swansea	3803	Columbine
587	Gramatan	710	Tecla	3804	Vanity
588	Oradell	712	Medean	3808	Aberdale
590	Rodista	714	Vanessa	3812	Tiara
592	Belvoir	716	Juno (also 103057)	3830	York
593	Roberta	723	Moselle	3840	Serena
603	Trojan	D1441	Sedan	3841	Toloa
604	Exeter (also 98834)	1802	No-name	3842	Hermosa
605	Fondale	2222	Gainsborough	3843	Mirabelle (also 114075)
608	Elvira (also 98835)	3004	Ransdell	3849	Dresalda
609	Lismore (also 98836)	3024	Redlace	3852	Lorento
610	Farney	3025	Touraine	3854	Valdina (also 112927)
611	Muriel (also 98838)	3031	Camelot (also 117817, repeat	3855	Marcia
613	Alcona (also 100326)		of 6000; shapes differ)	3860	Rigaud
614	Bayard	3052	Rosalie	3870	Grandeur (also 112930)

3871	Sierra	5053	Peony	13680	No name
3872	Annabel	5106	Madera	13714	Tokio
3886	Penrosa	5146	Remembrance	13857	The Malay
3903	Lynbrook	5147	Roselane	14369	Ormonde (Bassett)
3905	Kelvin	5153	Dulcy	14370	Carmen
3906	Harmony (also 117811)	5154	Maywood	14763	Inwood
3913	Stanwyck	5158	Therese	16033	Blue Willow
3914	Lilac	5215	Cordova	16034	No name; see 175 White and Gold
3915	Symphony	5220	Stanford		
3918	Magnolia	5224	Wilshire	19322	Azalea (also 252622)
3940	Sonora (also 117814)	5295	No name	20056	No name
3950	Camillia (also 4735, 117816, 117508)	5305	Shasta	26979	No name
		5316	Shelburne	35762	Alicia
3981	Goldenrose	5317	Somerset	42200	No name; called by some "Raised Gold"
3983	Goldfleur	5402	Carole		
4001	Acton	5524	Andrea	43061	(Same as 16034)
4003	Savoia	5528	Florence	44318	No name
4005	Lauritz	5558	Bluebell	58581	The Ceylon
4007	Lurline	5605	Margot	58584	Seville
4011	Cavatina	5612	No name	58588	The Alsace
4017	Berenda	5656	Garnet	58589	Beverly
4018	Queenanne	5767	Oxford	58590	The Sahara
4026	Ashford	5818	Stanwyck	58591	Florencia
4036	Adelpha	5860	Sanford	58593	Montclare
4049	Ackley	5924	Windsor	58594	Hanover
4070	Goldrina	6000	Camelot (same as 3031; shapes differ, also 117817)	58595	The Monterey
4706	Wrocklage			58596	Majestic
4715	Bluedawn	6002	Rosebud (not same as Melrose 6002)	58597	The Argonne
4716	Dresdoll			58598	Lafayette
4726	Cerulean	6003	Chevonia	58599	Coniston
4730	Greenbriar	6127	Fremont	61227	Tuscan
4731	Cardinal (also, same as 193; shapes differ)	6504	Ramona (also 1118708)	61228	Rochambeau
		6903	Kendal	61229	No name
4732	Carmela (also 95635)	7257	Revenna (also 109493)	61230	Chainrose
4733	Dresita	7267	Goldcella	61235	Laureate
4735	Camillia (also 3950, 117508, 117816)	7270	Revenna (nearly the same as 7257)	61237	Arleigh
				61239	Chanazure
4901	Naomi (same as 674; shapes differ)	7280	Mayfield	61241	Chantaro
4902	Nanarosa (same as 682; shapes differ)	7286	Goldette	68443	Bedford
		8035	Nadine	68445	Grosvenor
4907	Sonoda	9488	No name (old Blue and White)	68448	Atlanta
4914	Hawthorne	10733	Phoenix Bird	68454	Chanesta
4981	Valiere	11006	Blue Willow	68457	Chanlake
4985	Goldkin	11292	The Sedan	68465	Vassar
5007	Rosemary	11298	Hakone	68466	The Basel
5020	No name	11632	Valencia	68469	Lincoln
5038	Glendale	11657	The Linwood	68470	Savona
5041	Roselace	11874	No name (old Blue & White)	68478	Chandella
5047	Laurette	13672	Vitry	68483	Knollwood
5048	Rosemont	13673	Portland	68585	The Angora
5049	Margarita	13674	Regina	68587	Bellefonte (also 69539)

68596 Baroda	78049 Minaret	95641 Gloria
69531 Deerlodge	78053 Perseus	95642 Marlene
69533 Sheridan	78054 Perdita	95645 Arlene
69534 Beaumont	78057 Favorita	95649 Alvin
69535 Lasalle	80459 Romeo	95654 Arnaud
69538 Malvern	80460 Athlone	97893 Gainford
69539 Bellefonte	80461 Fairfax	97894 Galavan
69540 Amiston	80462 Visalia	97902 Allure (also 586)
69541 Mayville	80463 Castella	98141 Mimi
69542 Minerva	80466 Montebelle	98212 Acacia (also 509)
69543 Paisley	80467 Marilyn	98214 Loyalo
69544 Daventry	80553 Sedalia	98215 Charoma
69545 Navarre	80754 Elmonte	98217 Linden (also 525)
69546 Modesta	80755 Fairmont	98827 Gastonia
71219 Doris	81603 Severy	98829 Cardinal (also 193)
71225 Zenda	81857 Nordich	98834 Exeter (also 604)
71421 Calais	82450 Aubery	98835 Elvira (also 608)
71422 Granada	83366 Andalia	98836 Lismore (also 609)
71423 La Fleur	83367 Estelle	98838 Muriel
71424 Delhi	83374 Florola	98845 Garfield
71425 Cornwall	83377 Eltovar	98846 No name
71426 Delmonte	85202 Flodena	100326 Alcona (also 613)
71427 Rosewood	85963 Oxford	100331 Bluedawn (also 622, 4715)
71430 Pontiac	86196 Roseglow	101270 No name
71432 Chelsea (also Windsor)	86197 Ivanhoe	103007 Claire (also 657)
71433 Windsor	86198 Resilio	103008 Phoebe (also 659)
71436 Marigold	86199 Marcell	103009 Nerrisa (also 673)
71437 Gotham	86200 Farland	103034 Trianon (also 676)
71629 Rosemary	86205 Girardo	103057 Juno (also 716)
71854 Sheila (also Burma)	86209 Bantry	104529 Salvador (also 303)
74009 Parrician	86216 Monarch	108369 Alexis (also 3721)
74083 Paragon	87195 Goldinthia	108374 Coypel (also 3732)
76567 Grasmere	87196 Marcisite	108378 Ciro (also 3744)
76568 Croydon	87197 Cheramy	108380 Merlin
76582 Mayflower	87198 Corinthia	109493 Revenna (also 7270)
76593 Superba	89482 Kenwood	112927 Valdina (also 3854)
76831 Fleurette	89483 Arvana	112930 Grandeur (also 3870)
76832 Ybry	89484 Elaine	114075 Mirabelle
76833 Apollo	89485 Lanare	117508 Camillia (same as 117816, 4735, 3950)
76834 Juanita	89486 Milford	
76835 Romance	89492 Althea	117791 Rainbow
76837 Penelope	89501 Rubigold	117811 Harmony (also 3906)
76839 Floreal	89527 Vornay	117814 Sonora (also 3940)
76840 Romola	91602 Luxoria	117817 Camelot (same as 6000, 3031)
76841 Aeolian	95632 Valiere	
76842 Chineblue	95632 Galatea	117816 Camillia (same as 117508, 4735, 3950)
76965 Sorrento	95633 Garland (also D167)	
76972 Mariana	95634 Glenmore	118708 Ramona (also 6504)
77631 Fleurgold	95635 Carmela	252622 Azalea (also 19322)
78047 Biarritz	95638 Luray	
78048 Carltonia (also Amorosa)	95640 Tiffany	

Cup Shapes and Sizes Found in Early Patterns

These cup shapes are from the early days of manufacture. Not included are the postwar shapes, with the exception of cup shape M, which we do show because it is a more modern version of cup shape E (the old LaSalle shape.)

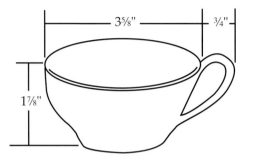

A. Probably the earliest shape. The size pictured is a teacup.

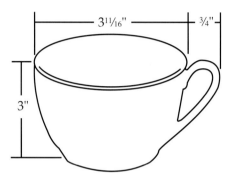

B. The coffee or breakfast size matching Cup A.

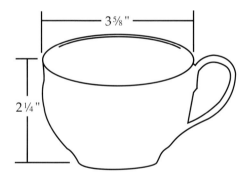

C. Another early coffee cup, often found in sets with Cup A teacups.

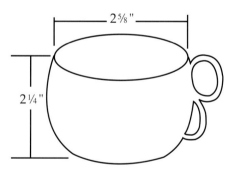

D. This double-handled teacup looks like a Bavarian shape but is found in early Noritake patterns.

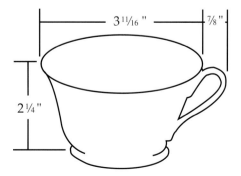

E. Teacup of the old LaSalle shape.

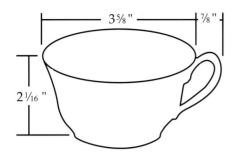

F. Teacup, another early shape. Same diameter as Cup A, but taller and has slightly more "bustle" shape.

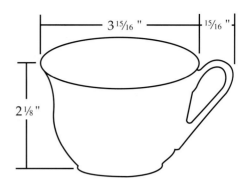

G. Coffee cup in same shape as Cup F.

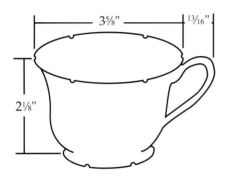

H. Teacup with scalloped top. This is the same blank as the demitasse in Cup W. Two-handled cream soups in this shape also have scalloped top.

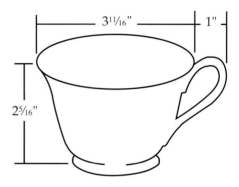

I. This is a modified LaSalle shape often found in sets of the Occupied Japan period. Slightly taller than Cup E.

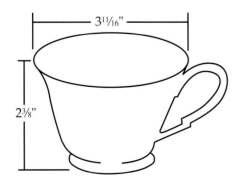

J. Same as Cup I, except for the handle. This cup comes with some patterns marked "shape design pat."

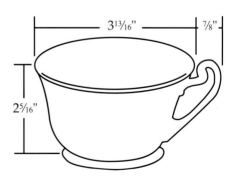

K. Another teacup with fancy handle.

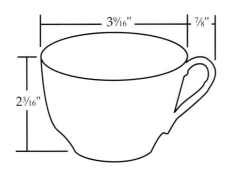

L. A modified and later version of Cup B.

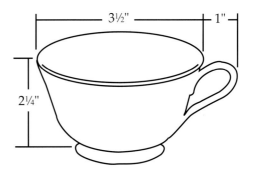

M. The LaSalle shape teacup, still in production. Note the heavier handle and larger size.

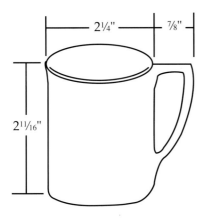

N. Chocolate cup.

O. Another chocolate cup. Please note that chocolate cups are taller than demitasse cups.

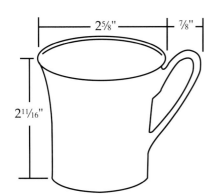

P. Chocolate cup. This one appears in a set of Goldena and so is an early shape.

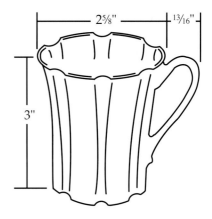

Q. Chocolate cup with scalloped top and base.

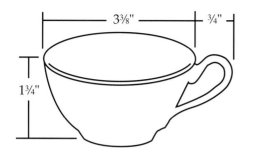

R. A cup made to fit the tea-and-toast tray.

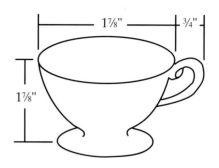

S. Footed demitasse cup.

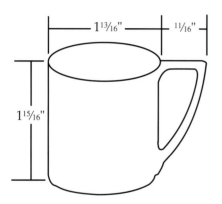

T. Demitasse cup found in set of 16034.

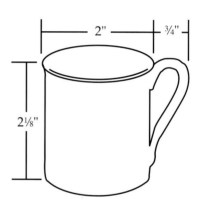

U. Another demitasse cup.

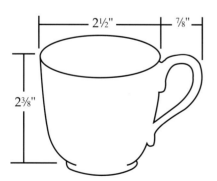

V. Unusual size for demitasse cup found with The Sedan.

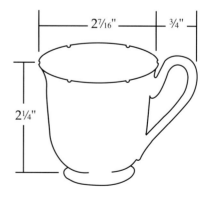

W. This is Cup H demitasse cup. Note difference in size.

Setting a retail value on pieces of early Noritake china involves considerable guesswork, since price has no relationship to the china's original cost or the price of the company's current patterns. Much depends on the extent of the demand for the piece and the pattern, the geographical area where it is found, whether a complete dinner or tea service is involved, and the source from which it can be obtained. In making a pattern identification, beware of going by name alone, for Noritake often used the same names on postwar patterns as on earlier patterns.

By and large, in a set or grouping, much depends on the particular pieces to be evaluated; a collection without cups and dinner plates, for instance, should not be valued as highly as a set that is more nearly complete. As a rule, patterns with names and/or numbers, being more easily identified, will command higher prices than those that must be matched by seeking out a sample for comparison. Bargains in patterns that show no name or number in the backstamp can still be found at estate sales, flea markets, and antique shops. Older patterns (from 1910 to 1925), particularly if they are named patterns, will bring more on the retail market than will later ones. A pattern that enjoyed wide distribution in the United States and is a popular pattern, including the Larkin premium patterns, will also command a greater price than one that is obscure. Of the older patterns, there are several that customarily bring a higher price than those less well known — and in these patterns there were many unusual pieces that now fetch a top market price. Such pieces include mint baskets, toothpick holders, ice cream sets, egg cups, jam jars, butter pats, chocolate cups and pots, coffee and tea sets, pancake dishes, syrup pitchers, ramekins and their underplates, and sugar shakers. It is always advisable to get an appraisal from a Noritake expert to assist you in determining a fair price, either for what you own or what you plan to buy.

Patterns from the 1930s usually did not include the truly rare pieces, but often did have square luncheon plates, bouillon cups, soup plates (sometimes two-handled cream soup bowls), oatmeal bowls, in addition to small fruit and berry bowls. Place settings often consisted of eight or nine pieces, rather than the five-piece settings sold in current designs. Customarily available as extras to the standard dinner set were demitasse pots and cups, teapots, and tea-and-toast cups and plates.

Named and numbered patterns from the 1930s until the outbreak of the war with Japan are extremely popular today, but as can be seen from the price schedule for these backmarks, they included fewer unusual pieces than the older patterns. Many of these patterns were reissued during the years immediately after World War II — often with no number or a different number.

Furthermore, postwar patterns were sometimes made on different shapes or blanks than were the originals, but the decals were identical to the earlier versions; often they can be successfully intermixed with the original patterns. Some dealers and collectors are particularly interested in finding sets marked "Made in Occupied Japan," because such a short interval is involved that they may increase in value at a greater rate than pieces of the same pattern not so marked.

To reach a judgement as to the value of a set or pieces of a set, one should first compare the backmark on china with its photograph in order to approximate the age of the pattern and to note its backmark number (or numbers). Many patterns will have more than one backmark given in the legend. This indicates that the pattern was manufactured either for a longer period of time than is now customary, or that it was reissued at a later date due to customer demand.

Some patterns produced for the Japanese market in the early days have enjoyed such popularity that they were continued in production, but with more recent backmarks, up until 1934; such is the case with Azalea and number 16034, the latter being current under the name White and Gold, but now numbered 175. Rare pieces in patterns such as these, with their wide span of backmarks, are to be found only on earlier versions.

Of course, all pieces must be examined thoroughly to ascertain that they are free of fractures, chips, scratches and wear of applied materials (silver, gold, et cetera) if they are to command top prices. Sets should contain an even number (usually 8 to 12) of each place setting piece, together with appropriate serving pieces.

One must be aware that frequently in older sets certain pieces are the ones most likely to be missing; i.e., cups and dinner plates are broken more often than other pieces. Therefore, a premium price must be expected for such items, while saucers for example, are proportionately of lesser value. When buying selected pieces to complete a set, one must expect to pay a per piece (premium) price.

Bear in mind that suggested prices represent a composite of values from many sources; undoubtedly, wide fluctuations will be found, occasioned by pattern popularity in various geographical areas. Remember, too, that some designs were manufactured only in tea sets, coffee sets, dessert sets and breakfast sets and did not include, for instance, dinner plates or large dinner serving pieces.

Those with unlisted rare or unusual pieces should seek the assistance of a specialist in old Noritake patterns in establishing a value.

SCHEDULE A

Patterns MM-1 through MM-18 (1891–1918)

Teacup, breakfast cup, $25.00 – 30.00.

Saucer for above, $7.00 – 9.00

Demitasse cup and saucer, $20.00 – 30.00 per set

Chocolate cup and saucer, $20.00 – 30.00 per set

Four o'clock tea cup and saucer, $25.00 – 55.00 per set

Dinner plate, $20.00 – 30.00

Luncheon plate, $20.00 – 30.00

Square luncheon/salad plate, $25.00 – 35.00

Salad plate, $15.00 – 20.00

Bread and butter or "pie" plate, $12.00 – 15.00

Soup bowl (7½"), $15.00 – 20.00

Two-handled bouillon cup and saucer, $25.00 – 35.00 per set

Two-handled cream soup (larger than bouillon), $25.00 – 35.00

Underplate for above soup, also used as a dessert plate, $12.00 – 18.00

Berry bowl (also called fruit or sauce dish), $10.00 – 14.00

Oatmeal bowl, $15.00 – 18.00

Covered vegetable tureen, oval or round, $85.00 – 125.00

Open vegetable, oval, round, divided, assorted sizes, $45.00 – 55.00

Large platter, 16" or more in length, $75.00–125.00

Medium platter, 13½"–14" in length, $60.00 – 75.00

Small platter, 11½"–12" in length, $40.00 – 60.00

Celery tray, $45.00 – 50.00

Pickle or relish dish, $35.00

Gravy boat, usually with attached tray, $50.00 – 60.00

Sugar bowl with lid (demitasse or standard), $40.00 – 50.00

Creamer (demitasse or standard), $30.00 – 40.00

Milk jug, $85.00 – 100.00

Waste bowl for tea set, $35.00 – 60.00

Covered butter, 3 pieces with dome, $45.00 – 65.00

Teapot, demitasse pot or chocolate pot, $90.00 – 150.00

Egg cup, $25.00 – 35.00

Lemon plate, $25.00 – 40.00

Candy dish or small nappie, $45.00 – 60.00

Larger nappie, $55.00 – 75.00

Three or four-part relish, $45.00 – 65.00

Syrup jug with underplate, $80.00 – 100.00

Mayonnaise set with underplate and ladle, $50.00 – 85.00

Jam jar, $50.00 – 75.00

Salt and pepper, depending on size, $40.00 – 50.00

Individual open salt trays, $15.00 – 25.00

Butter pat, $15.00 – 18.00

Chop plate, $55.00 – 75.00

Open-handled cake plate, $50.00 – 65.00

Two-piece pancake dish, $65.00 – 90.00

Tea and toast set (small cup with own tray), $25.50 – 35.00

Covered cheese dish, $50.00 – 75.00

Spoon holder, $40.00 – 50.00

Ice cream set (seven pieces), $300.00 up

SCHEDULE B

Patterns MM-19 through MM-26, also MM-28 (1918–1921)

Teacup, breakfast cup, $25.00 – 35.00

Saucer for above, $7.00 – 9.00

Demitasse cup and saucer, $25.00 – 35.00

Dinner plate, $20.00 – 30.00

Luncheon plate, $20.00 – 25.00

Salad plate, $15.00 – 17.00

Bread and butter, or "pie" plate, $12.00 – 15.00

Soup bowl (7½"), $15.00 – 17.00

Two-handled bouillon cup and saucer, $25.00 – 35.00

Two-handled cream soup (larger than bouillons), $25.00 – 35.00

Underplate for above soups, also used as dessert plate, $12.00 – 18.00

Berry bowl (also called fruit or sauce dish), $11.00 – 14.00

Oatmeal bowl, $15.00 – 18.00

Covered vegetable tureen, oval or round, $85.00 – 125.00

Open vegetable, various sizes, shapes, $45.00 – 55.00

Large platter, 16" or more in length, $75.00 – 125.00

Medium platter, 13½"–14" in length, $60.00 – 75.00

Small platter, 11½"–12" in length, $40.00 – 60.00

Celery tray, $45.00 – 50.00

Pickle or relish dish, $30.00 – 35.00

Gravy boat, $50.00 – 65.00

Sugar bowl with lid (standard or demitasse), $40.00 – 50.00

Creamer (any size), $25.00 – 35.00

Waste bowl for tea set, $35.00 – 60.00

Covered butter, 3 pieces, $50.00 – 70.00

Open butter tub, $45.00 – 55.00

Teapot, demitasse pot, or chocolate pot, $90.00 – 150.00

Egg cup, $25.00 – 35.00

Lemon plate, $25.00 – 40.00

Syrup jug with lid, $80.00 – 100.00

Covered mustard with spoon, $50.00 – 85.00

Salt and pepper set (depending on size), $40.00 – 50.00

Chop plate, $55.00 – 75.00

Open-handled cake plate, $45.00 – 65.00

Tea and toast set (small cup, own tray), $25.00 – 35.00

SCHEDULE C

Patterns MM-27 and MM-29 through MM-36 (late 1920's to early 30's)

Teacup, breakfast cup, $25.00 – 30.00

Saucer for above, $7.00 – 9.00

Demitasse cup and saucer, $25.00 – 35.00

Four o'clock teacup, pedestal base, with saucer, $25.00 – 55.00

Dinner plate, $30.00

Luncheon plate, $17.50 – 25.00

Square luncheon/salad plate, $25.00 – 35.00

Salad plate, $15.00

Bread and butter or "pie" plate, $10.00 – 12.00

Soup bowl (7½"), $15.00

Two-handled bouillon cup with saucer, $25.00 – 35.00

Two-handled cream soup (larger than bouillon), $20.00 – 35.00

Underplate for above soup, sometimes used as dessert plate, $12.00 – 18.00

Berry bowl (also called fruit or sauce dish), $12.00 – 14.00

Oatmeal bowl, $15.00 – 18.00

Covered vegetable tureen, oval or round, $85.00 – 125.00

Open vegetable, various sizes and shapes, $45.00 – 55.00

Large platter, 16" or more in length, $75.00 – 125.00

Medium platter, 13½"–14" in length, $60.00 – 75.00

Small platter, 11½"–12" in length, $45.00 – 60.00

Celery tray, $45.00 – 50.00

Pickle or relish dish, $25.00 – 35.00

Gravy boat, $55.00 – 65.00

Sugar bowl with lid (standard or demitasse size), $40.00 – 50.00

Creamer (any size), $25.00 – 35.00

Waste bowl for tea set, $35.00 – 60.00

Covered butter dish, three pieces, $50.00 – 70.00

Teapot, demitasse pot, or chocolate pot, $90.00 – 150.00

Egg cup, $20.00 – 30.00

Lemon plate, $25.00 – 40.00

Syrup jug with lid, $85.00 – 100.00

Three-piece sauce server with ladle and under-plate, $45.00 – 85.00

Salt and pepper set, depending on size, $40.00 – 50.00

Chop plate, $55.00 – 75.00

Open-handled cake plate, $45.00 – 65.00

Tea and toast set (small cup with own tray), $25.00 – 35.00

SCHEDULE D

Patterns MM-37 through MM-44 (1933–1940)

Teacup, breakfast cup, $25.00 – 30.00

Saucer for above, $7.00 – 9.00

Demitasse cup with saucer, $25.00

Four o'clock teacup with saucer, $25.00 – 55.00

Dinner plate, $20.00 – 30.00

Luncheon plate, $15.00 – 18.00

Square luncheon/salad plate, $25.00 – 27.50

Salad plate, $15.00

Bread and butter, or "pie" plate, $10.00 – 12.00

Soup bowl (7½"), $15.00

Two-handled bouillon cup with saucer, $25.00 – 30.00

Two-handled cream soup (larger than bouillon), $20.00 – 35.00

Underplate for above soup, also used as dessert plate, $12.00 – 18.00

Berry bowl (also called fruit or sauce dish), $12.00 – 14.00

Oatmeal bowl, $15.00 – 18.00

Covered vegetable, several sizes and shapes, $75.00 – 120.00

Large platter, 16" or more in length, $75.00 – 100.00

Medium platter, 13½"–14" length, $60.00 – 75.00

Small platter, 11½"–12" length, $40.00 – 60.00

Celery tray, $35.00 – 60.00

Pickle or relish dish, $25.00 – 35.00

Gravy boat, $45.00 – 60.00

Sugar bowl with lid (standard or demitasse), $35.00 – 50.00

Creamer (any size), $25.00 – 35.00

Waste bowl for tea set, $35.00 – 60.00

Covered butter dish, three pieces, $50.00 – 70.00

Teapot, demitasse pot, or chocolate pot, $90.00 – 150.00

Egg cup, $20.00 – 30.00

Lemon plate, $25.00 – 35.00

Syrup jug with lid, $75.00 – 100.00

Three-compartment jam dish, stand-up handle, $75.00 – 100.00

Three-piece sauce server, ladle and underplate, $50.00 – 85.00

Salt and pepper set, $40.00 – 50.00

Chop plate, $45.00 – 75.00

Cake and cookie serving plate, $50.00 – 65.00

Tea and toast set (small cup with own tray), $25.00 – 35.00

SCHEDULE E

Patterns MM-45 through MM-57 (1945–1964)

This group contains most of the "Made in Occupied Japan" patterns. There are fewer unusual and accessory pieces found here; however, since many of these designs are duplicates of earlier patterns, it is possible to add accessories from the earlier version, or vice versa.

Standard cup, $17.50 – 25.00
Saucer for above, $7.00 – 9.00
Demitasse cup with saucer, $20.00 – 30.00
Dinner plate, $18.00 – 30.00
Luncheon plate, $18.00 – 25.00
Salad plate, $12.00 – 15.00
Bread and butter or "pie" plate, $10.00 – 12.00
Soup bowl (7½"), $12.00 – 15.00
Berry bowl (fruit or sauce dish), $12.00 – 14.00
Covered vegetable tureen, oval or round, $75.00 – 120.00
Open vegetable, round or oval, $45.00 – 55.00
Large platter, 16" or more in length, $75.00 – 100.00

Medium platter 13½"–14" in length, $60.00 – 75.00
Small platter, 11½"–12" in length, $40.00 – 60.00
Pickle or relish dish, $45.00 – 55.00
Gravy boat, $50.00 – 60.00
Sugar bowl with lid, $40.00 – 45.00
Creamer, $25.00 – 35.00
Covered butter dish, 3 pieces, $40.00 – 50.00
Rectangular butter dish, 2 pieces, $35.00 – 40.00
Teapot or coffee pot, $75.00 – 110.00
Salt and pepper set, $35.00 – 45.00
Tea and toast set (small cup with own tray), $25.00 – 35.00

SCHEDULE F

Patterns MM-58 through MM-60 (1964 to present)

Standard-size cup, $18.00 – 25.00
Saucer for above, $7.00 – 9.00
Demitasse cup with saucer, $18.00 – 25.00
Dinner plate, $18.00 – 30.00
Combination luncheon/salad plate (8¼"), $12.00 – 14.00
Bread and butter or "pie" plate, $10.00 – 12.00
Soup bowl (7½"), $12.00 – 15.00
Soup/cereal bowl; often has mock handles, approximately 6½" diameter, $12.00 – 18.00
Berry bowl (fruit or sauce dish), $12.00 – 14.00
Covered vegetable tureen, oval or round, $70.00 – 95.00

Open vegetable, oval or round, $30.00 – 55.00
Large platter, 16" or more in length, $75.00 – 100.00
Medium platter, 13½"–14" in length, $65.00 – 75.00
Small platter, 11½"–12" in length, $40.00 – 50.00
Pickle or relish dish, $25.00 – 40.00
Gravy boat, $50.00 – 60.00
Sugar bowl with lid, $40.00 – 45.00
Creamer, $30.00 – 35.00
Two-piece rectangular butter dish, $30.00 – 40.00
Teapot or coffee server, $65.00 – 100.00
Salt and pepper set, $30.00 – 45.00
Tea and toast set (small cup with own tray), $15.00 – 25.00

SCHEDULE G

Patterns Azalea, Tree in Meadow, 16034, and 42200.

This schedule can also be used to approximate prices of rare pieces not heretofore seen in other early patterns. The piece numbers given refer to Azalea pattern, and are taken from the Larkin catalog of 1931.

2. Teacup, breakfast cup (Nippon-marked cups are lower end of schedule and are usually somewhat taller than Noritake-marked cups), $25.00 – 30.00
183. Demitasse cup with saucer, $150.00
     Chocolate cup and saucer, $80.00

13. Dinner plate, $35.00 – 40.00
338. Grill plate, $225.00
98. Luncheon plate, $35.00
315. Square luncheon plate, $75.00
4. Salad plate, $17.50 – 20.00
8. Bread and butter plate, $12.00 – 14.00
19. Soup bowl, $35.00
124. Bouillon cup and saucer, $35.00
363. Two-handled cream soup, $85.00
     (Azalea top of schedule)
9. Berry bowl or sauce dish, $14.00 – 15.00

55. Oatmeal bowl, $30.00
372. Covered vegetable, gold finial (Azalea), $480.00
101, 172, 12. Open vegetable, $60.00
439. Divided vegetable (Azalea), $150.00 up
311. Platter, 10¼", $175.00
56. Platter, 12", $40.00 – 45.00
17. Platter, 14", $65.00
186. Platter, 16" (Azalea), $400.00
99. Celery, $30.00 – 40.00
444. Celery (Azalea), $350.00
18. Relish, $20.00 – 30.00
119. Relish, four-compartment, $175.00
171. Relish, two-compartment, $50.00
450. Twin relish, loop handle (Azalea), $350.00
40. Gravy boat, $55.00
7. Sugar bowl with lid, $30.00
   Creamer, $30.00
123. Sugar and creamer set, $125.00
401. Sugar bowl, $75.00
   Creamer, $75.00
122. Sugar shaker and pitcher, waffle set, $150.00
449. Individual scallop w/sugar and creamer (Azalea), $400.00
100. Milk jug (Azalea), $200.00
310. Waste bowl for tea set, $70.00
314. Covered butter or cheese dish, $100.00
   Buttertub, fitted lid and insert (16034), $65.00
54. Buttertub, open, with insert, $45.00
400. Teapot, gold finial on lid, $500.00
15. Teapot, strap handle, $90.00
182. Coffeepot (Azalea), $375.00 up
   Coffeepot (Tree in Meadow), $375.00 up

120. Egg cup, $50.00
121. Lemon plate, $25.00 – 30.00
184. Bonbon plate, $150.00
193. Mint basket (Azalea), $150.00
97. Syrup jug with underplate, $150.00
3. Mayonnaise, three pieces, $35.00 – 50.00
453. Scalloped mayonnaise set, 3 pieces Azalea, $300.00
125. Jam jar with underplate, $120.00
88, 89. Salt and pepper, $40.00
26. Individual salt and pepper, $25.00
   Ball-footed salt (16034), $45.00
312. Butter pat, $50.00
10. Cake plate, $35.00 – 52.50
39. Tea and toast set, $35.00 – 47.00
189. Spoonholder, $75.00
191. Mustard, lid and spoon, $65.00
192. Toothpick holder (Azalea), $85.00 – 100.00
313. Tobacco jar (Azalea), $450.00
452. Bulbous vase (Azalea), $1,200.00
   Child's 15-piece set (Azalea), $500.00
   (Other patterns), $500.00
190. Cruet and stopper (Azalea), $190.00
169. Tea tile, $50.00
170. Compote, $120.00
185. Grapefruit dish (Azalea), $200.00
187. Fan vase (Azalea), (Tree in Meadow), $300.00 up
188. Shell dish (Azalea), $400.00
14. Condiment set, 5 pieces, $85.00
   Cracker and cheese (chip and dip), $150.00
   Ice cream set (16034), 7 pieces, $500.00 up

APPENDIX A: THE HOWARD KOTTLER COLLECTION

Before his death, we were extremely fortunate to have the permission of Howard Kottler, formerly of the University of Washington School of Art, to picture 15 designs of Noritake patterns from his personal library. These designs were created in the period from 1912 to 1920. We have been able to identify five of these by pattern name, by virtue of the fact that we have in our sample collection an actual piece of each that bears a name or number. The remaining ten are "mysteries." They may or may not have been put into production after the watercolors were submitted to the factory.

We cannot be sure of the significance of the numbers that appear on the drawings. These numbers are not the patent numbers, but are probably working numbers used to identify the designs between inception and production. Some of the letters are prefaced with the letter "D," which may stand for design, or for dinnerware. On the back of each original painting is a rubber stamp imprint that reads, "Not For Sale. Salesman's Use. Made in Japan."

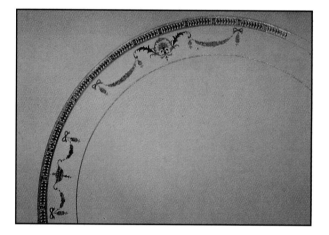

Figure 1: Sahara (1915)

Figure 2: Mandarin (1819)

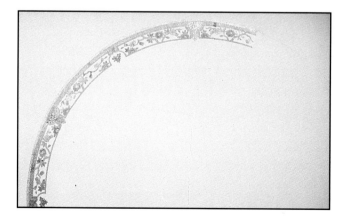

Figure 3: The Formosa (2008)

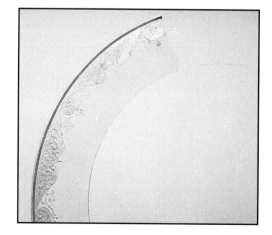

Figure 4: Unidentified (404)

Figure 5: Mystery 69 (2003)

Figure 6: Mystery 69 (Actual Sample)

Figure 7: Unidentified (1838)

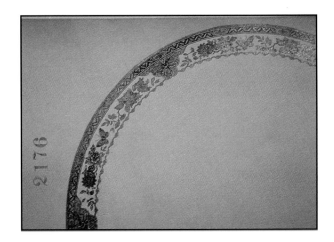

Figure 8: Unidentified (2176)

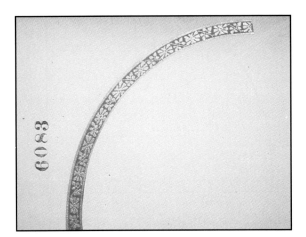

Figure 9: Unidentified (6083)

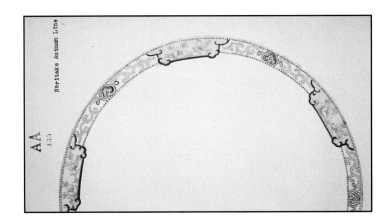

Figure 10: Unidentified (AA 435 Autumn Line)

Figure 11: Chantaro (2181)

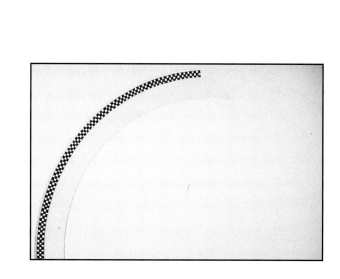

Figure 12: Unidentified (2004)

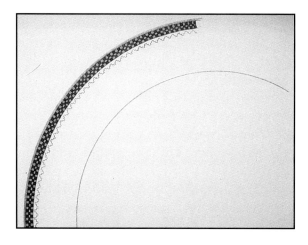

Figure 13: Unidentified (2120)

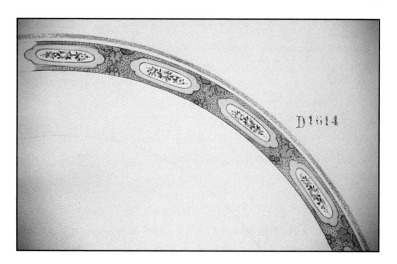

Figure 14: Unidentified (D1614)

Figure 15: Unidentified (D1714)

Figure 16: Unidentified (D1704)

The first settlers coming to America found no china here when they arrived, nor did they have the time or manpower to develop and maintain a prosperous ceramic industry for almost three hundred years. Small local potteries were set up early, but only for utilitarian wares; the vastness of the country and the distances between settled communities made the importation of clays and glaze materials difficult and expensive. The development of a china industry depended upon this as well as upon adequate supplies of fuel for firing kilns and water for the pottery-making itself, as well as for transportation of the fragile, heavy, and bulky finished product. The last but not least requirement was a good labor source. In Europe these needs could be and were being met, but the colonies were too busy carving a new nation from the wilderness to produce luxury goods such as fine china in the early days.

Since most of the first settlers were British and the early colonies had been financed and directed by English leaders and companies, most of the early tablewares came from England in English ships. Pieces were limited in type, consisting of mugs and tankards and crude, heavy pitchers and jugs. Setting a table as we know it today was unknown for over a hundred years!

To protect her china industry, England in the mid 1660s passed two Navigation Acts designed to prevent any European ceramic wares from entering England and her colonies except in English ships. The second act was an amendment to allow import, but only upon payment of import duties. A few wares, mostly useful ones, came in from Germany to the colonies, but there was little from the other European countries except that which entered through Canada or Spanish-held southern ports and French-owned Louisiana. These acts effectively limited anything except English chinawares from coming to their colonies until sentiment grew high against taxation without representation. The Boston Tea party, during which dissidents boarded an English ship and threw overboard a large cargo of Chinese tea in protest against the tax on tea, hastened the arrival of the American Revolution.

The first true porcelain was developed by the Chinese and introduced into Europe during the sixteenth century by Portuguese seafarers interested in the spice trade. At first, small amounts were brought in only incidentally as ship ballast, mainly to prevent the more precious spices and teas from being ruined by water seepage in the holds. This "china," as it came to be known, was composed of an almost white clay called by the Chinese "kao-lin" that, when glazed with "petuntse" or china-stone and fired in a hot kiln, fused and produced an almost translucent, very hard ware that could not be cut by a sharp instrument.

It was decorated first by underglaze painting in cobalt blue and later by overglaze painting in true enamel colors before being fired a second time at a very low temperature.

The introduction of this china into Europe led to the development in Italy of majolica. This clean, bright pottery was vastly superior to European wares then known, but it was still made from dark, heavy clays. It was easily broken, and the glaze chipped and cracked rather readily. However, this tin-glazed earthenware, or majolica, faïence, Delftware (Dutch) and delftware (English), as it later was known in various European countries, evolved into an attractive, soft, colorful pottery that continued as "top of the line" in Europe for many years. It is very collectible today.

By the beginning of the eighteenth century, Chinese porcelain was coming west in quantity, and the race was on in Europe to reproduce this ware. The earliest true porcelain was developed by a German named Böttger in 1717 working in Dresden under the patronage of the King of Poland. He came upon a substance that made it possible to work with white clay and keep it white after firing. However, he was never able to copy the fine potting and glazes of the Chinese wares. The French were making a soft paste porcelain by the mid century, as were the English and the Italians, but none of it could compare to that of the Chinese. Soft paste porcelain is made of kaolin but mixed with bone ash (in which case it is known as bone china) or some other ingredient rather than petuntse. This china is not as translucent as the hard-paste product, it must be fired unglazed and refired at a lower temperature, and it is not as hard. It has a softer look and usually very pleasing color combinations, the result of several firings.

The first true china clay or kaolin in America was discovered around 1732 in what later became the state of Georgia. Samples of a fine white clay were brought to the attention of General James Oglethorpe, leader of the Carolina Colony, and were sent by him to England. Examination of the samples by the leading potters in the Staffordshire district soon led to the realization that the same clays were to be found in the nearby counties of Devon and Cornwall.

English potteries with names well known today, such as Wedgwood, Leeds, Derby, Worcester, and Chelsea, were quick to take advantage of this discovery. Clay and later plaster-of-Paris molds were devised so that an endless variety of shapes and sizes could be made, leading ultimately to the setting of tables for the first time with services of china in every shape and size and for an unbelievable number of separate uses, including individual pickle dishes and asparagus servers, to name only two. By 1750, a new ware appeared. This salt-glazed stoneware was white, fine textured, light in weight, and durable. The English factories did not stop there. In the next fifty years, such well known and delightful chinawares as the English creamwares and pearlwares were introduced to an appreciative public.

All of this in no way slowed the China Trade, as commerce with China was then known. East India Companies were formed in Holland and England. Their ships sailed around the Cape of Good Hope and across the Indian Ocean, thus avoiding the Portuguese, to deal directly with the Chinese. Traders sailed as supercargoes aboard the sailing ships, and factories were set up in various port cities — mainly Canton, where the factors maintained warehouses and filled orders. The porcelain was made in inland China and brought down the rivers to be decorated. At first, decoration was in the Chinese manner, but it was not long before specific orders were being filled. European armorial devices were popular very early, and many of these sets ran into hundreds of pieces. Shapes were based largely upon samples of European silverwares that had been sent out to be copied. Blue-and-white patterns showing stylized scenes from nature were very popular. These led to the design by an English decorator-potter of

what have since come to be known as the "willow patterns," which were produced by the Chinese according to the specifications brought from England. These imports were soon known as Canton and Nanking wares. From the last decade of the eighteenth century, they came to America literally by the boatload.

By the end of the Revolution, American sailing ships were being designed with sleek lines that enabled them to sail with larger holds, carry more sail, and outrun and outgun almost anything else afloat. American privateers used this to advantage against the English during the War with Spain and later in the War of 1812.

Meanwhile America had grown and developed a prosperous middle class with tastes for the finer things, including Chinese porcelain. The Revolution had given impetus to the development of America's own Merchant Marine, and many merchant traders made the long voyage around the Horn and across the Pacific to Macao and Canton on the China coast. The first American vessel to undergo the rigors of the one- to two-year trip was the *Empress of China*, which sailed from New York in 1784. In the years following, a fierce rivalry developed among the merchant vessels, each captain trying to "clip" sailing time so as to be the first ship back with the goods. Lively races ensued between ships and countries. From around 1840 until the coming of steam American "clipper ships" came into their own. But English and Chinese chinawares were still better and cheaper than anything America was able to produce. The domestic china factories came, produced less attractive wares at high prices, and went!

Colonists had been arriving on American shores from other European countries since about 1650, beginning with a group that emigrated to Pennsylvania from Sweden, followed by the Dutch and a band of Mennonites. With the opening up of the South in Oglethorpe's Carolina Colony, French Huguenots and Salzburgers and Moravians from Germany arrived. The last two groups were later to develop significant pottery industries in North Carolina. America defeated the Spaniards in 1743 and took over Florida, purchased the Louisiana Territory from the French in 1803, and refought the British in 1812. New lands to explore and settle, new markets and manpower needs, and new waves of immigration!

In the 1840s the American china picture took on a new look. David Haviland, an American importer with a shop in New York City, had seen a cup from France that impressed him with its beauty and fine potting. In 1842 he opened a factory in Limoges, the center of the French kaolin-based porcelain industry, and established Haviland & Co. to produce porcelain designed for American export and American tastes. Other family members followed, and in time there were three separate Haviland factories in Limoges, all producing for the American market.

This gave new impetus to porcelain in America. Much of this French china was shipped directly to southern ports and traveled inland from there. Great quantities came in through Charleston, Savannah, and New Orleans, bringing fine china to what, not long before, had been the frontiers. For the first time there was fine porcelain made in quantity by an American, but it was not American-made.

The Far West was now calling more insistently than before with the discovery of gold in California in 1849 and the subsequent Gold Rush. The outbreak of war between the North and South in 1861 put a further strain on America's manpower, as the young men of both sides marched off to war. In 1869, the last spike was driven into the rails at Ogden, Utah, joining America from east to west with bands of steel. The discovery of gold and the coming of the railroads brought a wave of prosperity to the North, at the same time that the end of the Civil War, the subsequent period of Reconstruction and the boll weevil infestation of the cotton fields were impoverishing the South. This continued to be the picture for many years.

England was still taking up the slack in America's manpower shortage in the china industry. During the previous hundred years, great strides had been made in the development of tableware from lighter and whiter clays. A ware with a clear bluish glaze, finely potted, attractively decorated, and called "pearlware" was England's answer to the China Trade for almost 50 years. This was at first decorated with Chinese house designs mostly in blue. But later, scalloped, incised, or embossed border designs known as "shell" and "feather" edged china came into vogue. However, by 1820, pearlware was being superseded by an attractive, hard, white-bodied, white-glazed tableware that was neither hard nor soft paste but more of a "granite" or "stone china." Spode stone-china was introduced in 1806, and Mason's Ironstone in 1813, and the race was on!

This tableware filled the needs of the new, prosperous middle class in America. Their lifestyles did not call for true porcelain, but they wanted and could well afford to purchase a good, attractive, durable dinnerware. These English chinas filled the bill. Many of our ancestors had this "whiteware" and those of us who have inherited even a piece or two consider ourselves fortunate. It was well suited to a rural society, and much of America was exactly that during this period. The attractive scalloped shell and feather-edged patterns of the old pearlware are still here, in blue, green, and sometimes in wine or maroon. That this ware took America by storm is evidenced by the appearance even today of potsherds in corn, cotton, wheat and tobacco fields, along dirt roads, by riverbanks, lakeshores, and seashores when the water is low. Many pieces are found at old Indian village sites and around deserted slave cabins.

Transfer-printed patterns vied with shell edge in popularity, at first mainly in the blue willow designs, but soon in the historical wares showing American leaders, historical events, and classical sites and scenes from both sides of the Atlantic. These were decorated mostly in blue and known as Staffordshire "blue-and-white" to differentiate them from the earlier blue willow wares, but they also appeared in green, maroon, black, and sepia. American potteries were also producing some of these wares along with other styles in factories well known in America today but they were then making porcelain that was in no way competitive.

It was not until 1906 when Walter Scott Lenox organized the Lenox Co. in Trenton, New Jersey, to make fine, hard-paste, translucent, ivory-colored, true china that there was any appreciable competition on the home front. The Chinese export trade was still strong, and Nanking and Canton wares, as well as the "famille rose" or Rose Mandarin, and later Rose Medallion china, helped fill American china cupboards from east to west.

Then another country was heard from! The first Japanese porcelain known to have been taken to Europe was carried to the Netherlands in 1660, at a time when Dutch trade with China was interrupted because of Chinese domestic difficulties. However, this enterprise was short-lived, and in 1683 the Dutch resumed their China trading. Except for a few Portuguese emissaries and Jesuit priests, Japan continued its closed-door policy with the West until the signing of the trade treaty with America in 1858. It was not long before

American ships were visiting seaports of Japan, and fine Japanese porcelains began to be seen in America's drawing rooms. It is here that the Morimura clan, a farsighted and enterprising family with interests in chinaware, enters the picture. In 1878 The Morimura Bros. Co., later to become the Noritake Co. Ltd., embarked on a long and mutually profitable trade with the United States. When they began to export fine kaolin-based porcelain to this country they did not specialize in dinnerwares at first. Although China had long been filling the table service needs of the West, Japan had only recently brought an end to almost three hundred years of self-imposed isolation from western influences. There was much to learn and assimilate.

One incident will serve as an example. From the company's New York office in 1883, Yukata Morimura shipped a French-made coffee cup to Japan with the suggestion that the production of such cups be considered for the American market. Since most Japanese had never seen a handled cup, having been accustomed to handleless tea bowls, the impact of this can be well imagined. With true Japanese thoroughness and attention to detail, trips to France to study occidental table services and the production problems involved preceded the company's decision to embark wholeheartedly on making white, western-style porcelain dinnerware for America's tables. It would be interesting to know if the Japanese visited the Charles Haviland factory during their trip. They must have had with them someone who could speak English, and the English-speaking Havilands with their American china business would have been likely sources of information and assistance.

In 1904, the forerunner of the present Noritake Co. Ltd. was founded, and the company's first true dinner services reached America at about the time of the outbreak of World War I in 1914. America was busy — at first in aiding the European war effort — later taking her place in the fighting itself. Again imported china found a ready market in America.

During the years of peace that followed, Japanese export china found wide acceptance, especially in the postwar years of the Great Depression. Americans had little money to spend, but that did not mean that they did not crave nice things. And as before in history, the desires of the growing middle class were fulfilled.

Today we are accustomed to seeing bright, well-made pottery and chinas offered in our chain grocery stores — not for sale, but to be acquired as premiums for purchases. This marketing concept is not particularly new.

In 1876, John D. Larkin established a business in Buffalo, New York, that had a long-lasting effect on American life. He began by selling bath and laundry soap, but rather than marketing through stores, he went directly to the consumer in what he called "factory to family" sales. To stimulate sales, customers were given coupon "dollars" that equaled the amount of their purchase. Housewives saved Larkin coupons (and bought lots of Larkin soaps) so they could acquire the item of their choice "free of charge" from the Larkin premium catalog.

By 1900 the company had grown phenomenally. In 1909, Larkin catalogs listed 900 premiums that included drug products, perfumes, tea, coffee, extracts, paint products, and even furniture and accessories. The Buffalo Pottery was established by Larkin to produce chinawares of various kinds and, from 1904 to 1925, a line of dinnerware patterns.

By the 1920s, as postwar American production costs soared, the Noritake Co. had begun producing an export line of porcelain dinnerware patterns, some of which were designed exclusively for Larkin. These included Azalea and Raised Gold. Others, such as Linden, Briarcliff, Savoy, Modjeska, and a scenic pattern in fall colors known as Tree in the Meadow, were also offered by Larkin. By 1940, as the post-Depression economy picked up and more people had cars and better roads to get to town, the Larkin Company went out of business. By this time other companies had entered the mail-order business, and chain stores dotted the land.

The New York office of the Noritake Co. Ltd. closed in 1940 shortly before the United States entered World War II. For five years its factory in Japan produced little chinaware — and that only for domestic consumption. However, in 1945, production was resumed on a less limited scale, and dinnerware was available to occupation forces and post exchange personnel. By the mid 1950s, the familiar Noritake name was again seen in china departments and on dinner tables throughout the country. A quote by an American executive of the Noritake Company pretty well sums it up: "Noritake — born in Japan, raised in America, enjoyed by the World!"

BIBLIOGRAPHY

Alden, Aimee Neff and Richardson, Marian Kinney. *Early Noritake China*. Lombard, Illinois: Wallace-Homestead Book Co., 1987.

Bagdade, Susan and Al. "Answers on Antiques." *The Antique Trader*, November 7, 1984.

Cox, Warren E. *The Book of Pottery and Porcelain*, Vol. II. New York: Crown Publishers, 1946.

Coleman, Dorothy S., Elizabeth A., and Evelyn J. *The Collectors Encyclopedia of Dolls*. New York: Crown Publishers, 1968 and 1986.

Donahue, Lou Ann. *Noritake Collectibles*. Des Moines, Iowa: Wallace-Homestead Book Co., 1979.

Gaston, Mary Frank. *The Collector's Encyclopedia of Limoges Porcelain*. Paducah, Kentucky: Collector Books, 1980.

Hume, Ivor N. *A Guide to Artifacts of Colonial America*. New York: Alfred A. Knopf, 1970.

Kottler, Howard. *Noritake Art Deco Porcelains*. Pullman, Washington: Museum of Art, Washington State University, 1982.

Melvin, James and Florence, and Bourdeau, Rodney and Wilma. *Noritake Azalea China*. Danbury, Connecticut: Red, White and Blue Shop, 1975.

Meyer, Florence E. *The Colorful World of Nippon*. Des Moines, Iowa: Wallace-Homestead Book Co., 1971.

Miyakawa, T. Scott. *Pioneers of Japanese American Trade, Their Struggles and Triumphs*. Privately printed, 1970.

Noritake Co. Ltd. *The History of Noritake and Noritake History of the Back Stamp*. Brochure, 1981.

————. *List of Pattern Names*. By number, February 20, 1966. Privately circulated.

————. *Supplement to List of Pattern Names* (Post-war Patterns). By alphabet, January 1, 1976. Privately circulated.

————. *Supplement to List of Pattern Names* (Post-war Patterns). By alphabet, April 1, 1982. Privately circulated.

————. *Supplement to List of Pattern Names* (Post-war Patterns). By number, April 1, 1982. Privately circulated.

————. *Supplement to List of Pattern Names* (Post-war Patterns). By alphabet, July 1, 1991. Privately circulated.

————. *Supplement to List of Pattern Names* (Post-war Patterns). By number, July 1, 1991. Privately circulated.

Oates, Joan Collett. *Phoenix Bird Chinaware*. West Bloomfield, Michigan: Oates, 1985.

Quimby, Ian M.B., ed. *Ceramics in America*. Winterthur Conference Report. Charlottesville, Virginia: The University Press of Virginia for the Henry Francis DuPont Winterthur Museum, 1982.

Robinson, Dortha. *Hand-painted Nippon China*. Manchester, Vermont: Foreward's Color Productions, Inc., 1972.

Schiffer, Nancy N. *Japanese Porcelain*. West Chester, Pennsylvania: Schiffer Publishing, Ltd., 1986.

Smith, Patricia R. *Antique Collector's Dolls*. Paducah, Kentucky: Collectors Books, 1975.

Stitt, Irene. *Japanese Ceramics of the Last 100 Years*. New York: Crown Publishers, 1974.

Van Patten, Joan F. *The Collector's Encyclopedia of Nippon Porcelain*. Paducah, Kentucky: Collector Books, 1979.

————. *The Collector's Encyclopedia of Nippon Porcelain, Second Series*. Paducah, Kentucky: Collector Books, 1982.

————. *The Collector's Encyclopedia of Noritake*. Paducah, Kentucky: Collector Books, 1984.

Wojciechowski, Kathy. *The Wonderful World of Nippon Porcelain, 1891 – 1921*. West Chester, Pennsylvania: Schiffer Publishing, Ltd., 1992.

COLLECTOR BOOKS

I n f o r m i n g   T o d a y ' s   C o l l e c t o r

For over two decades we have been keeping collectors informed
on trends and values in all fields of antiques and collectibles.

BOOKS ON POTTERY, PORCELAIN & FIGURINES

4927	**ABC Plates** & Mugs, Lindsay	$24.95
4630	American **Limoges**, Limoges	$24.95
4844	**American Painted Porcelain**, Kamm	$19.95
4929	**American Art Pottery**, 1880–1950, Sigafoose	$24.95
1312	**Blue and White Stoneware**, McNerney	$9.95
1958	**Blue Ridge Dinnerware**, Revised 3rd Ed., Newbound	$14.95
1959	**Blue Willow**, Revised 2nd Ed., Gaston	$14.95
4848	Ceramic **Coin Banks**, Stoddard	$19.95
4851	Collectible **Cups & Saucers**, Harran	$18.95
1373	Collector's Encyclopedia of **American Dinnerware**, Cunningham	$24.95
4931	Collector's Encyclopedia of **Bauer Pottery**, Chipman	$24.95
4932	Coll. Ency. of **Blue Ridge Dinnerware**, Vol. II, Newbound	$24.95
4658	Collector's Encyclopedia of **Brush McCoy Pottery**, Huxford	$24.95
5034	Collector's Ency. of **California Pottery**, 2nd Ed., Chipman	$24.95
2133	Collector's Encyclopedia of **Cookie Jars**, Roerig	$24.95
3723	Collector's Encyclopedia of **Cookie Jars**, Volume II, Roerig	$24.95
4939	Collector's Encyclopedia of **Cookie Jars**, Book III, Roerig	$24.95
4638	Collector's Encyclopedia of **Dakota Potteries**, Dommel	$24.95
3961	Collector's Encyclopedia of **Early Noritake**, Alden	$24.95
5040	Collector's Encyclopedia of **Fiesta**, 8th Ed., Huxford	$19.95
4718	Coll. Encyclopedia of **Figural Planters & Vases**, Newbound	$19.95
1439	Collector's Encyclopedia of **Flow Blue China**, Gaston	$19.95
3812	Collector's Encyclopedia of **Flow Blue China**, 2nd Ed., Gaston	$24.95
2086	Collector's Encyclopedia of **Gaudy Dutch & Welsh**, Shuman	$16.95
3813	Collector's Encyclopedia of **Hall China**, 2nd Ed., Whitmyer	$24.95
3431	Collector's Encyclopedia of **Homer Laughlin China**, Jasper	$24.95
4946	Collector's Encyclopedia of **Howard Pierce Porcelain**, Dommel	$24.95
1276	Collector's Encyclopedia of **Hull Pottery**, Roberts	$19.95
3962	Collector's Encyclopedia of **Lefton China**, DeLozier	$19.95
4855	Collector's Encyclopedia of **Lefton China**, Book II, DeLozier	$19.95
2210	Collector's Encyclopedia of **Limoges Porcelain**, 2nd Ed., Gaston	$24.95
2334	Collector's Encyclopedia of **Majolica Pottery**, Katz-Marks	$19.95
1358	Collector's Encyclopedia of **McCoy Pottery**, Huxford	$19.95
3963	Collector's Encyclopedia of **Metlox Potteries**, Gibbs	$24.95
3837	Collector's Encyclopedia of **Nippon Porcelain**, Van Patten	$24.95
2089	Collector's Ency. of **Nippon Porcelain**, 2nd Series, Van Patten	$24.95
1665	Collector's Ency. of **Nippon Porcelain**, 3rd Series, Van Patten	$24.95
4712	Collector's Ency. of **Nippon Porcelain**, 4th Series, Van Patten	$24.95
5053	Collector's Ency. of **Nippon Porcelain**, 5th Series, Van Patten	$24.95

1447	Collector's Encyclopedia of **Noritake**, Van Patten	$19.95
1037	Collector's Encyclopedia of **Occupied Japan**, Vol. I, Florence	$14.95
1038	Collector's Encyclopedia of **Occupied Japan**, Vol. II, Florence	$14.95
2088	Collector's Encyclopedia of **Occupied Japan**, Vol. III, Florence	$14.95
2019	Collector's Encyclopedia of **Occupied Japan**, Vol. IV, Florence	$14.95
2335	Collector's Encyclopedia of **Occupied Japan**, Vol. V, Florence	$14.95
4951	Collector's Encyclopedia of **Old Ivory China**, Hillman	$24.95
3964	Collector's Encyclopedia of **Pickard China**, Reed	$24.95
3877	Collector's Encyclopedia of **R.S. Prussia**, 4th Series, Gaston	$24.95
1034	Collector's Encyclopedia of **Roseville Pottery**, Huxford	$19.95
1035	Collector's Encyclopedia of **Roseville Pottery**, Vol. 2., Huxford	$19.95
4856	Collector's Encyclopedia of **Russel Wright**, 2nd Ed., Kerr	$24.95
4713	Collector's Encyclopedia of **Salt Glaze Stoneware**, Taylor	$24.95
3314	Collector's Encyclopedia of **Van Briggle** Art Pottery, Sasicki	$24.95
4563	Collector's Encyclopedia of **Wall Pockets**, Newbound	$19.95
2111	Collector's Encyclopedia of **Weller Pottery**, Huxford	$29.95
4853	Collector's Guide to **Camark Pottery**, Gifford	$18.95
4942	Collector's Guide to **Don Winton** Designs, Ellis	$19.95
4860	Collector's Guide to Homer Laughlin's **Virginia Rose**, Racheter	$18.95
3434	Coll. Guide to **Hull Pottery**, The Dinnerware Line, Gick-Burke	$16.95
3876	Collector's Guide to **Lu-Ray Pastels**, Meehan	$18.95
3814	Collector's Guide to **Made In Japan Ceramics**, White	$18.95
4646	Collector's Guide to **Made In Japan Ceramics**, Book II, White	$18.95
2339	Collector's Guide to **Shawnee Pottery**, Vanderbilt	$19.95
4954	Collector's Guide to **Souvenir China**, Williams	$19.95
4734	Collector's Guide to **Yellow Ware**, McAllister	$17.95
1425	**Cookie Jars**, Westfall	$9.95
3440	**Cookie Jars**, Book II, Westfall	$19.95
5265	**Lefton China** Price Guide, DeLozier	$9.95
2379	Lehner's Ency. of **U.S. Marks** on Pottery, Porcelain & China	$24.95
4722	**McCoy Pottery**, Coll. Reference & Value Guide, Hanson	$19.95
5268	**McCoy Pottery**, Volume II, Hanson/Nissen	$24.95
4726	**Red Wing Art Pottery**, 1920s–1960s, Dollen	$19.95
5055	**Red Wing Art Pottery**, Book II, Dollen	$19.95
1670	**Red Wing Collectibles**, DePasquale	$9.95
1440	**Red Wing Stoneware**, DePasquale	$9.95
3738	**Shawnee Pottery**, Mangus	$24.95
4629	Turn of the Century **American Dinnerware**, Jasper	$24.95
4572	**Wall Pockets** of the Past, Perkins	$17.95
3327	**Watt Pottery** – Identification & Value Guide, Morris	$19.95

This is only a partial listing of the books on antiques that are available from Collector Books. All books are well illustrated and contain current values. Most of these books are available from your local bookseller, antique dealer, or public library. If you are unable to locate certain titles in your area, you may order by mail from COLLECTOR BOOKS, P.O. Box 3009, Paducah, KY 42002-3009. Customers with Visa, MasterCard, or Discover may phone in orders from 7:00–5:00 CST, Monday–Friday, Toll Free 1-800-626-5420. Add $2.00 for postage for the first book ordered and $0.30 for each additional book. Include item number, title, and price when ordering. Allow 14 to 21 days for delivery.

Schroeder's
ANTIQUES
Price Guide

. . . is the #1 bestselling antiques & collectibles value guide on the market today, and here's why . . .

8½ x 11, 608 Pages, $12.95

- *More than 450 advisors, well-known dealers, and top-notch collectors work together with our editors to bring you accurate information regarding pricing and identification.*

- *More than 45,000 items in almost 550 categories are listed along with hundreds of sharp original photos that illustrate not only the rare and unusual, but the common, popular collectibles as well.*

- *Each large close-up shot shows important details clearly. Every subject is represented with histories and background information, a feature not found in any of our competitors' publications.*

- *Our editors keep abreast of newly developing trends, often adding several new categories a year as the need arises.*

If it merits the interest of today's collector, you'll find it in *Schroeder's*. And you can feel confident that the information we publish is up to date and accurate. Our advisors thoroughly check each category to spot inconsistencies, listings that may not be entirely reflective of market dealings, and lines too vague to be of merit. Only the best of the lot remains for publication.

Without doubt, you'll find
SCHROEDER'S ANTIQUES PRICE GUIDE
the only one to buy for
reliable information and values.

COLLECTOR BOOKS
A Division of Schroeder Publishing Co., Inc.